NIGHTMARE ABROAD

NIGHTMARE ABROAD

Stories of Americans Imprisoned in Foreign Lands

BY PETER LAUFER

Foreword by
John G. Healey
Amnesty International USA

Mercury House
San Francisco

Published in the United States by
Mercury House
San Francisco, California

United States Constitution, First Amendment: Congress shall make no law respecting an establishment of religion, or prohibiting the free exercise thereof; or abridging the freedom of speech, or of the press; or the right of the people peaceably to assemble, and to petition the Government for a redress of grievances.

Frontispiece: One of the few Americans jailed in post-Communist Eastern Europe looks out to the streets of Prague from Ruzyně prison. (Photo: Randall Lyman)

Mercury House and colophon are registered trademarks
of Mercury House, Incorporated

Printed on recycled, acid-free paper
Manufactured in the United States of America

Library of Congress Cataloging-in-Publication Data
Laufer, Peter.
   Nightmare abroad: stories of Americans imprisoned in foreign lands / by Peter Laufer.
   p. cm.
   ISBN 1-56279-028-5
   1. Prisoners—United States.   2. Prisoners—Foreign countries.   3. Americans—Foreign countries.   I. Title.
HV8706.L38   1993
365'.6—dc20   92-15811
                                                                              CIP

5 4 3 2 1

Again, with love to
Sheila
for the continuing inspiration
and the lessons in freedom

Also by Peter Laufer

Iron Curtain Rising
A Personal Journey through the
Changing Landscape of Eastern Europe

Contents

Foreword

John G. Healey
Executive Director
Amnesty International USA

Governments jail people who commit legally proscribed offenses against society. In theory, this way of doing things seems reasonable. In real life, the practice often gets out of hand. It ensnares countless people throughout the world in the machinery of state terror. It strips some people of their basic human rights and costs others their lives.

When the United Nations convened after World War II, the governments of the world decided to set limits on state powers to control and coerce individuals. The government delegates argued and cajoled, insisted and compromised, and came up with the *Universal Declaration of Human Rights.* This declaration, proclaimed without dissent by the United Nations General Assembly in 1948, is the foundation of today's international humanitarian law. It's an impressive document. If you ever need to be inspired, read it. Our world would be much more just and peaceful if governments' practices were consistent with their pledges to uphold the terms of the declaration.

From my perspective as executive director of Amnesty International USA, it seems that government systems of incarceration tend to break down in any or all of five critical areas. In most countries, official tolerance of a breakdown in one area leads to abuses throughout the criminal justice system.

Arrest: Government agents, according to international law, aren't allowed to simply walk around a town or drive around the countryside and arrest anyone who strikes them as undesirable. The Universal Declaration states, "No person shall be subjected to arbitrary arrest or detention. No one shall be deprived of his liberty except on such grounds and in accordance with such procedure as are established by law."

Fair and prompt trial: If government authorities take you into custody, you have the right to be told the reason for your arrest and to challenge the legality of your detention before a court of law. Assuming that you're properly charged and then brought to trial, you have the right to adequate defense and to fair proceedings.

In other words, governments break international laws when they do not bother to tell you why they've picked you up, when they force you to stay in jail for a prolonged period without a trial, or when they speed you through some mockery of justice and stamp Guilty on your file.

Conditions of imprisonment: You're entitled to humane treatment. Shackling a naked prisoner to the floor is not humane. Neither is starving prisoners or denying them adequate medical treatment. Yet this kind of thing is done in every region of the world. It's barbaric, and it's illegal.

Torture: This is absolutely, unequivocally forbidden. Under no circumstances may interrogators or prison guards or any other government agents torture you. That's the law. And in over half of the world's countries, this law is broken. Torture, like the other human rights abuses I've mentioned, does not have to happen. If government leaders demonstrate the political will to stop torture, the people employed by the state will stop it. It's as simple, and as complex, as that.

Punishment: There's a lot of leeway in this area, as I suppose there must be. No punishment, however, should cross into the realm of cruel and inhuman treatment. Amputating limbs is cruel and inhuman. Killing a prisoner who is already secured in state custody is cruel and inhuman. No matter who you are or what you've done, you have rights to life and to protection from brutal treatment.

The laws of some sixty countries still permit the death penalty, although not all of these countries actually kill prisoners. Every year more countries abolish this bloody remnant of a previous era. The United States is the only Western industrial country that continues to kill prisoners.

Fundamental human rights such as the ones outlined above are not privileges that states may award a person for good behavior or deny a person for bad behavior. They're birthrights. Peter Laufer has done us

all a service by vividly describing what can happen when governments
abnegate their human rights obligations.

In some places, people risk their lives to demand basic rights. At the
very least, we who live in freer societies should protest human rights
abuses on behalf of those who cannot.

Everything west of Istanbul is just a suburb of L.A.

American adventurer Milan Melvin,
in a 1973 letter from his home
in Kathmandu to the
author, in Paris

We always took care to make it understood that we were Americans—Americans!

Mark Twain, *The Innocents Abroad,* 1869

I cannot rightly tell how I entered it, so full of sleep was I about the moment that I left the true way.

Dante Alighieri, describing passing into hell
in *The Inferno,* 1318

Around the World

Man is born free, and everywhere he is in irons.

Jean-Jacques Rousseau,
The Social Contract, 1762

|||||||||||||||||| For work and pleasure, more Americans are traveling than ever before. It's easy and cheap to jump on an airplane and in just a few hours land in a culture far away from home. Millions of Americans are seeing the world, from day trips to Tijuana or Montreal to jaunts to exotic ports of call, like Bangkok, Karachi, Lima, or Moscow.

Too often, Americans believe the privileges and rights of U.S. citizenship follow us wherever we go, that the cavalry will come charging to our rescue if we're bothered by foreign authorities or violate foreign laws.

It's just not so, as the thousands of Americans enduring a rugged life in foreign jails show. Average, law-abiding Americans are susceptible to unexpected encounters with other nations' judicial systems, encounters that too often result in sudden and miserable jail time. Innocent travelers find themselves locked up for months and years, their friends and families unable to pry them loose from unsympathetic foreign jailers. Among the stories compiled in these pages are the nightmares of a tourist from Maryland who was jailed in Greece after charging a few hundred dollars over his Visa credit-card limit, a Texas oil worker who languished in a Saudi Arabian prison charged with importing pornographic videotapes, an Illinois college student who was imprisoned in Czechoslovakia for distributing Bibles, a New Jersey businesswoman who faced the Nigerian death penalty for breaking a retroactive trade law, and a man who crashed his car after driving from California into Mexico and remained behind bars during the accident investigation. These are stories that prove an experience in a foreign prison can befall any American.

1

Even the raw statistics compiled by the State Department bear this out. At the beginning of 1992, for example, fifteen Americans were listed as having been arrested the year before for violating fishing regulations somewhere in the world. Seven were arrested for tax law offenses, thirty-two spent time locked up on vagrancy charges, and a worrisome seventy-eight were detained for crimes listed as "unknown" by the State Department.*

High in a drab office building on the Virginia side of the Potomac across from Washington is a mock-up of a dingy jail cell. There future U.S. foreign service consular officers try to learn how to deal with the problems Americans can face overseas. I watch one day as an actress – a really convincing young woman, crying and hysterical – plays the part of an arrested American, and a consular officer-in-training works on his future role.

She is sobbing as he enters the cell. The room, lit by harsh lamps, is painted gray and covered with graffiti. There is a plain table and two chairs. Two small, barred windows and a clock on the wall complete the set.

"May I sit down?" he asks. She sniffles in acquiescence. "I'm sorry we couldn't get here sooner," he tells her, adding, "We've been very concerned about you."

She responds in a scared, hollow voice, asking, "Who are you?"

"I'm the vice-consul from the American embassy. My name is Richard Adams."

Confused and upset, she responds, "Why are you here now? Why? I wanted somebody for so long. I don't know who you are."

"I want to help you," he says calmly. "We understand it's been quite a while since you've been here. We've tried to come and see you. We tried to come." She just sobs, and he says quietly, "It's terrible," and then asks, "Where are you from in the United States, Natalie?"

"I'm from Kansas," she sobs. It is only a training role-playing session, but it sends chills up my spine. The setting is so realistic, the actress so believable, that after just these few moments, observers of the interview feel the terror and helplessness of a stranded prisoner.

"You're from Kansas?"

*These statistics appear in the State Department Bureau of Consular Affairs's *Report to Congress on Americans Incarcerated Abroad,* the most complete record available. It is published annually by the State Department's public affairs office in Washington, D.C.

"Yeah, that's where my mom and dad are."

"Are your parents still there?"

"Yes, yes," she chokes between the crying. "Can you get my parents?" It is a plaintive plea. "Can you bring my parents?"

"We'd love to get in contact with your parents for you."

"Can you bring me my mom?" she interrupts. "I—I need to talk to my mom."

"We will do our best to try and contact your parents, Natalie." He carefully promises nothing.

"I need my mom."

Then he makes his move to get around the Privacy Act. "We need your permission before we contact your parents." She cries. Without a Privacy Act waiver, the consular officer is precluded by federal law from disclosing anything about the plight of a specifically named adult prisoner, even to the immediate family. "Natalie, is it all right with you if I write down some notes of our conversation so that I can make sure I have information and send it correctly to your parents."

"You won't tell the guards, will you?" She's scared.

"No, this is confidential, between you and me."

"Everything's fine, everything's fine here. Everything's fine. I didn't tell you anything."

"Whatever you tell me, it's just between you and me."

"Okay."

"Now, where are you from in Kansas, Natalie?"

"My mom and dad, and me," her voice cracks, "we live in Middleton, Kansas."

"Is that very far from Lawrence? I have some friends who went to school in Lawrence."

"You know Kansas?"

"I've never been there, I'm from Wisconsin. But I had some friends who went to school there."

Suddenly she cries out again, "Are you gonna bring my mom and dad to me? That's where they are!"

"I'll try and get in touch with them," he says again.

"They're in Kansas," she wails. "My dad will get me out of here. He'll help you. He will."

"Okay. I haven't seen your passport. The authorities here have your passport. Is there any information about where your parents live in your passport?"

"Yes. My dad will help me, too. You get my dad, okay?"

"Okay," he says, "we will call your mother and your father."

"Why did you come now?" she asks again.

"We've been trying to come for a long time."

"You can't trick me," she interrupts. "I've never seen you before, but if you're a guard, I told you everything, I don't know what else to say. I didn't do anything. I didn't! And Bernardo was with me!" More tears. "But he wasn't there when you woke me up."

"Who is Bernardo?"

"Bernardo is my friend."

"Natalie, do you know where we are? Do you know which country we're in?"

She cries more, "They kept saying I was in Z. I wasn't. I wasn't. I went to Y. I was in Y. I've always been there."

"How long have you been in Y?"

"I don't know why I'm here." Her answers come between cries and sobs.

"Can you remember when you went to Y?" he asks.

"Yes, I've been traveling for months, now. I've been here three weeks."

"Were you traveling in Y? What kind of things were you doing?"

"I met Bernardo. Where is Bernardo?"

"I don't know who Bernardo is. Is Bernardo a friend?"

She stops crying for a second, worried. "Maybe they hurt Bernardo, too. But he wasn't there when they woke me up."

"Is Bernardo an American?"

"No, Bernardo's from Y."

"Were you and Bernardo on a trip?"

"The day before I came here, Bernardo said, 'Natalie, do you want to go on a picnic?' And we did that before." Then in an outburst, she adds, "Just because Bernardo's friends wore what they did! I didn't know."

"Tell me about his friends a little bit."

"His friends wore army outfits. I guess they had guns. But I didn't know they were bad men. Are they bad men?"

The exercise continues until eventually it is determined that Bernardo used Natalie's camera to take pictures of not just her, but also a building. They fell asleep, and she was kicked awake by her captors. Bernardo was gone and she was taken to prison, raped, and beaten. The trainee gets Natalie's signature on the waiver and says he'll get word to her parents and will return the next day with money, food, and more information about her case.

It is an impressive performance, even if it is just a practice session with an audience.

Marin County, California, where I live and grew up, is an island of privilege, one of the richest enclaves in the world. The basic transportation route for traveling up and down the county is U.S. 101, a commuter's freeway that snakes over the hills and through the valleys, past million-dollar homes and luxury shopping centers. I find myself on 101 just about every day. Northbound traffic often backs up on the filled-in marshland just south of the Corte Madera Creek. On the west side of the freeway looms Mount Tamalpais and its promise of wild beaches and the Pacific; dominating the view off to the east are the high walls of San Quentin Prison.

There is an alternative to sitting stuck in the traffic. Marin commuters to San Francisco can relax on sleek ferryboats that sail from the mouth of the Corte Madera Creek at Larkspur Landing. Over hot coffee and pastries, we can read the morning paper as the boat eases slowly from its dock past San Quentin, so close we can make eye contact with the prisoners, who sometimes smile and wave from their confinement.

My close neighbor San Quentin is a constant reminder that the ultimate luxury is freedom. I've only been locked up a few times, and only for a short period each time. Once it was in Sausalito, for unpaid parking tickets. I was held in the little cage in the Sausalito police station until the clerk calculated the total fines I owed. It was a couple of hundred dollars, as I recall. But for some reason, I happened to be carrying a wallet full of cash that day, and I paid up and walked out.

Another time, some overzealous San Francisco police came bounding into an apartment I was renting after they spotted something suspicious-looking on the front porch. Guns drawn, they dragged me off to the station. The LSD and peyote possession charges were thrown out as soon as the police laboratory confirmed my claim that the powder they found was actually tapioca pudding mix and the weird-looking wrinkled things in a bag were dried peaches.

I've been incarcerated outside of America, too; again, just briefly. Twice when I was crossing the border between East and West Germany, I was stopped and locked in holding cells while my papers were thoroughly checked. I was interrogated and the contents of my pockets inspected. Both times I was let off with a sharp warning; once not to attempt to practice journalism in East Germany without a permit, the other time after my contraband copy of the *International Herald Tribune* was confiscated and thrown in the trash.

I was also held by the Turkish army along their border with Armenia. It was right after the 1988 earthquake, and I was reporting on the damage to Turkish villages. Outside of Kars, I made my way up a dirt road to a bluff overlooking the destroyed Soviet city Leninakan. What I failed to realize was that I had crossed into a restricted military zone, and for the next several hours I was guarded by a Turkish soldier who smiled, offered me endless cups of tea, but wouldn't let me go until his commanding officer was satisfied that my press credentials were legitimate and that I understood his stern warning to stay away from the border.

My experiences behind bars have been painless and brief, but undoubtedly contributed to my curiosity about life in jail, especially foreign jails. Just those hours of being denied the liberty to walk elsewhere was a stark lesson to me of how restricting it is to be locked up, especially in a foreign culture under substandard conditions, and particularly if you didn't know you did anything against the law, or don't believe that you did anything wrong.

To investigate such a nightmare abroad, I traveled around the world, stopping in twenty-one countries to visit Americans. Despite resistance from most foreign jailers and even some U.S. consular officials, I managed to tour prisons. I talked with American prisoners, U.S. and foreign government officials, and Americans released from custody, now safely back home in the States. It is not a pretty story.

In the tropical heat outside Bangkok, I yelled back and forth across wire mesh and bars with an American in his tenth year of a thirty-year sentence. "I am a defeated person," he told me, and he looked like a man with no hope.

In the Philippines, jailers laughed, telling me Americans don't stay locked up in that former U.S. colony. They simply flash dollars when they're caught breaking all but the most serious laws, pay for any damages they cause, and buy their way out of custody.

I saw filth surrounding an American woman in a Pakistan prison, modern lockups in Germany and France that looked escape-proof, comfortable places in Canada where prisoners feel lucky to be far from violent U.S. prisons, and a Mexican prison where money can buy just about anything.

I chose my route by seeking a cross-section of the types of conditions facing Americans. I was looking for convicts locked up for a variety of reasons. And I prepared for the trip by verifying – as best I could – that there was a reasonable chance I could get into a country's prisons before I added that country to my itinerary.

It was a fascinating, sobering, and instructive tour. Readers must remember, though, that governments, policies, and laws are constantly changing. Some of the specific conditions described in these pages may change radically from one day to the next. What experience clearly teaches is that every day, somewhere in the world, unprepared Americans are unexpectedly encountering police, prison, and court conditions extremely different – and often terrifyingly worse – than our own. This is not a xenophobic or nationalistic statement; it is simply a reporting of the facts.

Should Americans be paranoid beyond their borders and never leave home? Of course not. But a basic knowledge of local laws is more important to take along on a foreign journey than a voltage converter, a phrase book, or a change of clothes.

Beans or Luxury in Tijuana

One of their favorites is carbonated water. What
they do is gag you so that you can't breathe through
your mouth and they shake the bottle and when the
water escapes, it goes up your nose on the inhale.
They continue this until your lungs feel like they've
been filled with water and you get to the point
where it's—"Stop! Whatever you want to hear,
whatever you want me to sign."

La Mesa inmate Darrel Hall describing
the torture that led to his confession

Nobody beats a sentence in Mexico unless they've
got a lot of money to pay off judges, lawyers, cops,
you name it.

Former Mexican prisoner Patrick Allen Tate
in Juarez, en route home

This jail does not offer any security against escape.
If we haven't had more escapes it is because the
prisoners don't want to, but they sure could do it
any time.

Warden of the Tijuana City Jail after
three prisoners sawed through the bars and
escaped down a rope

|||||||||||||||||||| **A**mericans stand out in the crowds on Avenida Revolu-
ción in Tijuana as conspicuously as the street-corner donkeys that are
so curiously painted to look like zebras. The vendors bark their wares
at the gringos; the cabs cruise by slowly, the drivers yelling.

"Taxi?" asks still another cabbie.

"No," is the answer.

"You want woman?" is the next question. It is easy to get into trouble in Tijuana. Trouble is one of Tijuana's most profitable industries.

South from the tourist strip that hugs the international frontier, the nightclubs and trinket stands give way to upholstery shops, car dealers, and a residential district. There, miles from the tawdry downtown but still within sight of the hills of San Diego County north of the border, La Mesa Penitenciaria waits for the unlucky, including plenty of Americans.

"I had a car accident." Keith Prohaska doesn't mind his name being noted. He has been locked up in La Mesa for three weeks, charged with drunk driving and destruction of private property: the parked cars he hit. But he talks like a prison veteran: "You learn real quick, Spanish is not the language here. Money is."

We are standing around the noisy open yard inside La Mesa; I am meeting the handful of Americans held in the Baja California Norte state penitentiary. Keith still sounds dazed when he speaks of his sudden confinement. "I had several drinks at dinner. I don't know how long I've got here." He is already disgusted with his own government. "The American consul is absolutely useless. All they do is call home collect and give us vitamins."

Alex Hines is a little more than a third of the way through his seven-year sentence for possession of one gram of marijuana and contributing to the delinquency of a minor. "It was just seeds," he complains. "If I had killed somebody I would have been out already." For almost two of his years inside La Mesa, Alex's wife and two young children lived in the prison with him. "Oh yeah, my wife was here. Every day she'd go out, go to the store, shop, do what she had to do, do laundry, whatever, come back in. We'd walk around the field."

A counterfeiter joins the group, a marine serving five years – he's been in eleven months so far – and allows that life isn't so bad for him, considering he is in prison. "There are certain benefits you can't get in the States: women and bottles."

Another marine agrees. "This is a better jail than jail in the States. Let me put it this way: If you've got the money, you can get anything you want."

"Except out," interrupts Phil Trembley who says he has been locked up for a year, and then looks at his watch and adds, "and eleven days."

The charge is homicide, but Phil has not yet been tried, let alone convicted and sentenced.

More Americans are behind bars in Mexico than in any other foreign country, probably because so many Americans travel south of the border naively looking for fun and profit. According to the State Department, a third of all the Americans arrested abroad are detained in Mexico, and the numbers grow year after year. In 1991, 1,050 Americans were arrested in Mexico; in 1990, that number was 941, dramatically more than just a few years before. That means 1,050 Americans made official contact with the Mexican criminal justice system. Many more were arrested and quietly managed to bribe their way out of trouble before they arrived downtown and became statistics. Some of the arrests were merely inconveniences, dealt with smoothly, with the disturbed American out of custody quickly. But by the end of 1991, a total of 613 American citizens were still locked up south of the border, wandering around Mexican prison yards like the one I visited at La Mesa, and now even the State Department admits that many of those American prisoners are physically and psychologically tortured.

"I couldn't believe it. I thought this had to be a nightmare," recalls Darrel Hall, an American who had been arrested in Tijuana. His detention turned into over a year behind the walls of La Mesa. "I went from shock, to disbelief, to fear. I realized that basically on an accusation from one person you can be locked up for an indefinite period of time."

The high walls of La Mesa don't keep the outside world away from the convicts, they just keep the inmates away from the outside world. Guards armed with rifles crouch on top of those walls, looking sinister in their blue jeans, T-shirts, and baseball caps. There is something especially threatening about their lack of official uniforms, a reminder that the authority they represent does not necessarily answer to a government that controls them. They look like free-lance toughs, adding to the sense of whimsical justice that pervades the Mexican legal system.

One guard is on the ground at the front gate of the prison, working alone. The gate is a far cry from the sophisticated automatic barriers complete with detection equipment protecting prisons in Canada, France, and Germany. At La Mesa, it's just a swinging door in the chain-link fence. The gatekeeper casually cradles a machine gun and watches over a steady stream of visitors coming and going, deciding who comes in and who doesn't, decisions based as much on deals and bribes as on legalities. Any searches of the visitors are cursory operations. That's why inmates can buy just about anything they want or need inside the prison.

A small clutch of Mexicans is outside the gate, mostly women, talking rapidly, gesturing, passing parcels. Inside, the yard is full of prisoners and a blaring loudspeaker barks orders, announcing visitors and calling individual inmates.

The warden is expecting me, as I called ahead. He looks elegant in his suit and tie and makes me struggle with his language before breaking into an English that's much more proficient than my Spanish. Behind him are four shotguns in a case scattered with boxes of shells. He smiles and offers me free run of his teeming institution.

This warden is new to the job and probably decided when I asked for the tour that allowing a reporter on the grounds would be valuable for the tarnished image of La Mesa. The previous warden has just been in all the local newspapers after a shoot-out in a downtown Tijuana bar. He and some friends had stopped in at the Hawaiiano Bar at the Palacio Azteco Hotel for a bout of pretty serious drinking. One of the men got angry when the bartender said he was getting too drunk and should go home. The drunk fellow pulled a 22-caliber pistol and started shooting up the bar. The former warden grabbed for the gun and – according to the accepted story – it went off accidentally and killed the drunk. The warden was reassigned to a job with a lower public profile.

Behind his office, in an open alleyway leading to the yard, the new warden has collected La Mesa's American inmates, all eager to talk. Their stories come fast, tumbling out all at the same time, all rejecting the American government as worthless to their causes. None of the inmates know when they are getting out of La Mesa, but all agree that they are being treated better than most other inmates because they are Americans with money.

We walk into the yard, which looks like a stage set for a small, poor Mexican village. The inside of the actual prison wall is difficult to see. In most places it is covered by what the Mexican inmates call their *caracas,* private quarters referred to as "houses" by the Americans. And indeed they are houses, tiny but adequate private rooms actually built onto the prison's walls. For an American with images of American-style prisons as a reference point, these private homes inside the walls are disorienting. Furnished with shag rugs and TV sets, equipped with padlocks controlled by the inmates, they bring to mind children's club-houses more than prison cells.

"I did all of this," one of the marines says, proudly showing off his studio apartment, barely larger than his bed. An English-language San Diego television station is coming in loud and clear on the black-and-white set. "I did all of this, even the wiring." Where did he get the wire and the connectors and the electrical outlet? "A hardware store delivered it."

Some of the houses are on a second floor, complete with balconies, barbecues, and a sweeping view of the nearby San Diego hills.

"At first it was really scary," says Alex Hines, the inmate serving seven years for marijuana possession. "But then—I dunno—I haven't been in touch with friends of mine or the normal way a person is supposed to live. Just being locked up in here, it's just like, hard. It's bad."

But soon he learned to deal with his new routine. "I get up, eat, go with a few other Americans who are in here, you know, we just talk. That's about it. Watch TV. Listen to the radio. Walk to different places back and forth in here, to different cells people are living in in here. And that's about it. And then go eat, go to sleep, and occasionally, like when I have visits here, like when my wife's here and stuff, we go eat and, you know, everything else you could probably do on the outside."

Alex's house sports two bedrooms, a bathroom, and a kitchen. He has room for a couch and apologizes for the mess, but the Mexican woman prisoner who cleans for him hasn't arrived this day from the women's side of the prison. From his smile and wink, it is clear she performs other services for Alex, too, when his wife isn't visiting or living with him. We run into his "maid" later in the women's section of the prison. They hug and hold hands while we talk. The guard escorting us hoots over the hand holding; Alex just smiles. Cooking, cleaning, and prostitution are the most common options available to the women inmates for making money in the prison economy.

The women live in a separate wing of the prison, but mingle with the men as they go about their daily business. Carol, one of the American women in La Mesa, sits on her cell floor chewing a pear as we talk. "Stay out of Mexico," is her advice. "Especially if you have tattoos. They saw my tattoos." Carol is accused of robbery, a charge she denies. So far, she has been locked up for eight months of pretrial detention.

"They don't do much of anything to help," she says of the U.S. consular officials. "They just ask what's happening. I'd like them to give us a lawyer from over there. These lawyers are jokes."

|||||||||||||||||||||| The courtyard has a village atmosphere; but unlike the frivolous stay made famous by the Kingston Trio popular song, many Americans experience years of tedium punctuated by moments of violence in Tijuana's La Mesa Penitenciaria. (Photo: *San Diego Union*, James Skovmand)

Carol looks tough and seems in her element sitting on the cell floor. "I'd done a robbery," she says as she explains her history in Tijuana. "I got out, went back to the U.S., came back here to drink with some friends of mine. I was only here three days." Then she was picked up for robbery again.

"I've been hit because I wouldn't cop to the robbery," she tells me in a resigned voice. "I'm waiting to go to court to see how much money they want. It all works on money."

"It's pretty well set up," Alex says proudly about his house. "You'd be surprised, this is like no prison at all. This is like, they just take me off the street, and they put me in another world, but away from everyone else. And I have to get along with all these people in here." Getting along with his neighbors is important for self-preservation. He tells stories of stabbings and killings in La Mesa. "I never thought about death until I came here," he says. But on the high-rent side of the prison where his and the other Americans' *caracas* are scattered, life is relatively quiet. The really nasty fights and fires usually occur across the yard in the maximum security section of the prison, or where the poorest prisoners share unlocked cells. "Where I live, it's fine. It all depends on how you're set, financially. If you've got a lot of money you can do anything here."

Alex Hines's *caraca* cost him about five hundred American dollars to secure and furnish. For the duration of his sentence, it's his. And he didn't need to come up with all of the money up front. The prison administration takes time payments for the house. Alex and the other inmates either buy what they need from the outside, get it from visiting friends and relatives, buy it through the prison marketplace, or do without. Nothing is free. Even the routine beans and rice from the prison kettle require a payment to the guards.

Mordidas these daily expenses are called, literally "little bites." Everything carries a price: blankets, cots or the more comfortable beds, showers, and, of course, illegal recreation like drugs, alcohol, and sex. The guards provide the goods, take a cut for themselves, and augment the warden's salary with his percentage. This controlled, market-driven economy keeps prison costs low for the government, and makes the job of guard and warden appealing because there is plenty of extra money to be made for those who know how to use the system. Mexican and other Latin American politicians point with some pride to their prison systems, saying that because they approximate life on the outside they are a more humane method of incarceration and better prepare inmates for their return to open society than the greater isolation of North American penal communities.*

Prisoners with no money sleep outside in the yard. Even one of the unbarred barren cells, known as the Tanks, costs twenty-five cents a night. Women with babes in arms mingle with their men in the Tanks and throughout the prison. Only the most incorrigible are locked up behind bars in the the cellblock called *Las Tombas,* the Tombs.

Radios blare pop music throughout the prison yard, competing with the official announcements coming over the loudspeakers. A couple of smiling men sashay by flirtatiously, their faces heavily made up, their cheap women's clothing ill-fitting.

"If you're a clean person, you can stay clean," explains one of my guides as we pick our way through the rougher and dirtier neighborhoods of La Mesa, "If you're a pig, you can live like a pig." A guard tags along as we tour, but he just smiles; he doesn't censor the commentary, nor does he keep me from seeing the entire complex. "The guards are really good people," says Alex. "Once you're in here, it's okay." He smiles, "there's a problem getting out." The guard smiles, too. He struts a bit, in stylish uniform and dark glasses, looking cool and comfortable. He's clearly feeling just as at home as Alex.

The Americans order out to Tijuana restaurants or grocery stores for their food, or eat at one of the restaurants in the yard owned and operated by inmates. These are actual private eateries. Coming into La Mesa for the first time, it takes some getting used to, these restaurants and the private apartments. The jail doesn't appear to be a penal institution as much as a walled city. I expected to find miserable prisoners and dirty facilities. I expected to hear horrible stories of abandonment and abuse from the Americans I found detained in Mexico. But the commercial village environment is an odd surprise.

The open-air restaurants are complete with hand-painted signs, just like those seen out in the streets of Tijuana. *Cantina,* announces one restaurant's brightly colored signs. Up on the makeshift wall is a listing of hamburgers, fries, and other menu offerings. The counter, too, is restaurant-issue Formica. Commercial bottles of catsup are set out with the meals, along with restaurant-style napkin dispensers. Inmate cus-

---

*More details on the socioeconomic conditions at La Mesa Penitenciaria can be found in *Tijuana: Urbanization in a Border Culture,* by John A. Price, published by the University of Notre Dame Press in 1973.

tomers and guards sit on red Naugahyde-covered swivel stools. A juke box pumps tunes out into the yard. For a minute it's possible to forget that this is a dangerous, dirty prison.

In the prison kitchen, where the inmates without the money to buy better meals get their food, the huge cooking tubs are bubbling with lunch."Every fucking time," says a Mexican inmate in English when he sees me taking notes,"beans and rice. Every fucking time, beans and rice." Alex and my other American guides point to the beans and rice with disgust and say they never eat the prison food.

We pass the bakery with its giant earthen oven, and the furniture shops, where exquisite parquet tables are produced along with other traditional Mexican folkcrafts. Private concerns contract with the warden to use the pitifully underpaid convict laborer to make the appealing handicrafts hawked for bargains in the stalls on the tourist-rich Avenida Revolución. This prison labor is a reality to consider when buying souvenirs in Tijuana. All the prisoners, including the Americans, must work—making pennies a day—unless they spend a few more pennies to bribe themselves out of their appointed jobs. Even roll call, *lista,* can be slept through; all an inmate must do is spend twenty-five cents "buying your count." There is a handball court, a movie theater (the pictures are always in Spanish), and a basketball court full of men shooting hoops.

Alex Hines and his colleagues are making the best of their bad situation at La Mesa, but the sometimes acceptable conditions do not mean that these Americans are happy. "I'm never going to come back to Mexico again," says Alex, musing about his release. "Never." And he goes back to a game of Risk with his friends, dreaming of taking advantage of the prisoner transfer treaty between the United States and Mexico. It's not that he would necessarily prefer to serve out his time in a U.S. prison. But once back north of the border, he could apply for parole and he knows that few U.S. parole boards would keep him locked up for seven years for the crime of holding one gram of marijuana.

Presidents Ford and Echeverria negotiated the prisoner exchange treaty. Military and political prisoners cannot take advantage of it, nor can inmates locked up for violating immigration laws. And once Americans accept a transfer, the Mexican conviction remains on their records; the right to appeal is lost. Those who serve out their sentences in Mexico can come home with a blank record in the United States. But, since the treaty was ratified, for thousands of Americans it's been a reprieve from the bizarre and dangerous conditions in which too many unfortunates find themselves trapped far from home.

"I was in a bar." Marine Phil Trembley, the La Mesa inmate behind the walls one year "and eleven days," is telling his story. He speaks about his crime with resignation, contemplating a long prison sentence once he is tried and convicted, and assuming he will be expelled from the marines too, once he finally gets back to the States. "Somebody slipped me some drugs. They tried to rob me and I killed somebody. Okay?" Cruising U.S. servicemen in Tijuana are high-profile targets for hustlers. Often they report that Tijuana policemen – sometimes in uniform, sometimes in plainclothes – pick them out of the crowds and threaten to arrest them unless immediate cash bribes are paid.

Like so many people locked up, Phil feels wronged. "Whether I'm guilty or not, there's a lot of extenuating circumstances. I'm going to say my hand did it, but I'm going to say I feel, personally, that it was self-defense."

Phil's story is typical. He was picked up by the police, he says, and then abused. Now he languishes in prison, wishing that his own government would do more to help him out of his predicament.

"I was beat and electrocuted and locked in a little room for the first five days I was in Mexico," he says coolly. "The first three days no one knew where I was at, including myself. I didn't even know what part of Mexico I was in. I was cold. My clothes were completely ripped. They had electrocuted me. They tied wires to my testicles. They put it up my nose. They beat me. You know, they beat me in the eyes and the kidneys, where there were no marks."

Phil says it was three days before the shore patrol and the U.S. consul showed up with a few blankets. "I got in trouble the last day in January and you can imagine how cold it was. I was in a little cell and there was defecation about five inches deep and I was handcuffed with my hands behind my back for three days solid, day and night. So I slept with handcuffs on, in defecation. In the mornings, the Mexicans, when they brought my food, it was two corn tortillas with some beans in the middle, they threw it in my cell. I wasn't allowed fresh drinking water; we drank water from the tap. I was so sick, I was terribly sick."

It is a common scenario Phil Trembley describes as he portrays the immediate post-arrest period experienced by Americans in Mexico. Even

U.S. government officials, so often careful to avoid alienating a foreign government by defending some individual American who complains about mistreatment after an arrest, acknowledge that the Mexican horror stories are a reality.

"I've heard so many horror stories that some of them must be true," is how Robert Ramos, an assistant federal public defender in El Paso, puts it. Ramos is often on hand to receive American prisoners taking advantage of the transfer treaty to come home. "One of the main reasons our government went along with the treaty was because of mistreatment of American prisoners."

The statistics maintained by the U.S. government are depressing, and lend credence to the stories told by individual inmates like Phil. In 1991, over half of the reports of mistreatment at the hands of foreign jailers came from Americans incarcerated in Mexico. Only about a third of Americans arrested worldwide that year were arrested in Mexico. Over the past several years, more allegations of mistreatment of Americans in foreign prisons came from those in Mexican jails than from those incarcerated in the rest of the world.

The routine seems to be simple. The police rough up whomever they arrest, extracting the signature they need for a confession. Then, once the American—and the same ritual plagues Mexicans—shows up in court, the signed confession is the prosecutor's Exhibit A.

"Mistreatment of American prisoners in Mexico continues to be a serious problem," states the Bureau of Consular Affairs in its 1990 annual report on American prisoners. "The overwhelming majority of mistreatment cases in Mexico involves persons accused of drug offenses. Various forms of physical and psychological torture are reportedly practiced, including beatings, electric shock, and threats of death."

The U.S. government has formally protested to the Mexican government but admits, "Authorities have been slow to respond. We will continue to urge the Mexican government to focus on this problem, but it may not be easy to break the cycle of widespread abuse which has been present for so long."

By 1991, the report was slightly more optimistic. The raw numbers were lower; 78 prisoners complained of torture, beatings, and other forms of intimidation, down from 124 the year before. These statistics can be quite deceiving. Often prisoners fear making a formal statement about mistreatment, worrying that such a report will encourage further abuse from their jailers or even adversely affect their court proceedings.

Nonetheless, the State Department attributes the decline "to the efforts by consular officers, who closely monitor arrest cases, and the cumulative impact of formal and informal protests filed when mistreatment occurs." Perhaps of even more importance to the future health and safety of Americans arrested in Mexico is a change in the law. Confessions are now admissible in court only when they are witnessed by the defendant's lawyer.

Certainly all the Americans arrested in Mexico are not innocent of wrongdoing. Especially just across the border in Tijuana and along the beaches of Baja California, many Americans come south looking for the questionable kinds of excitement involving drugs, drink, and sex. But if their behavior results in arrest, they face a much different philosophy about the role of the criminal justice system than exists back home. It's a system that accepts bribery, torture, and terror as part of the police process.

"The tourists who get arrested in Rosarito are cowards," the district attorney for that beach community just south of Tijuana told a reporter with disgust."When they are detained, they seem to be very macho types. But the day after being behind bars, they cry for their parents and they don't remember the trouble they've caused."

"I was sick, man, I was throwing up," Phil is still telling the story of those first days after his arrest. The U.S. Navy started shipping him bag lunches so he wouldn't be forced to eat jail food. "I had diarrhea, I was freezing at night, I was cold. I had to fight to get a bed, to get a place to sleep; thankfully I'm large enough that I did win out. I got a place to sleep."

After his arraignment, Phil was moved to La Mesa to face an open-ended period of incarceration while the authorities put together their case against him. This period of pretrial detention is common all over the world, and a harsh surprise for Americans accustomed to a judicial system that considers citizens innocent until proven guilty.

Much of the rest of the world operates under entirely different sets of principles. In Mexico, and most of Latin America and Europe, the Napoleonic Code is in effect, a legal system that seems to presume anyone suspected of wrongdoing by the police is guilty until and unless innocence is proved in court.

Again unlike in the United States, in Mexico and many other ports of call for Americans around the world, prisoners rarely are afforded the opportunity to bail themselves out of confinement during this period of pretrial investigation by the police and prosecuting lawyers. Detention without conviction commonly lasts from six months to over a year. Then comes the trial. If the prisoner is convicted, the so-called preventative detention (to prevent any flight from prosecution) is deducted from any prison time to which the inmate is sentenced. But if the verdict is not guilty, if the American charged with a crime is innocent, there is no compensation for the time spent locked up.

Almost all of the official complaints made by Americans to their own government about mistreatment at the hands of Mexican authorities cite abuse during the initial arrest and the interrogation that immediately follows. Once the prisoners start to languish in detention, the worst physical offenses are usually over.

Marine Phil Trembley was resigned but frustrated with his period of preventative detention when we talked in Tijuana. "At times," he said of La Mesa, "it's more than acceptable. At times it's comparable to Disneyland here. But at times it's like something out of Dante's *Inferno*. I mean, I've gone through a riot here where I've had guys try to rob me and actually had to engage in combat with a piece of wood just to protect my house and myself. Really. The guards, they all just stood and watched and were laughing and throwing tear gas at people. About a month ago they had a state police search in here and they were just like SS storm troopers. It was twelve o'clock at night. I was in bed. I don't have a lot of extra clothes, so I sleep naked. They come flying into my house, kick the door open. And a man's got an Uzi submachine gun and he's yelling at me – of course I don't speak Spanish, right – he's yelling at me. I say, 'Wait, I want to put my pants on.' And I reach to put my pants on and he slapped me. They play a lot of games with you that are really not necessary."

Phil is an entrepreneur. He runs one of the hamburger stands operating as private restaurants inside the walls of La Mesa. "Best burger around," he smiles. "I don't like to ask my family for money," he explains. "I have a wife and a son. I worked out a system where I can make enough money to keep them here in Mexico, if I work about fourteen hours a day." His family lives near the prison in an apartment.

Phil then uses his restaurant as an example of the bizarre economics at work inside Mexican prisons. "Basically I have a restaurant and I sell food, right? But all the food that I sell I have to buy through the prison, through the administration. So they get about an eight percent kickback right there. Because I buy the food from them, it's about eight percent higher. Now after I sell the food, each month I have to pay the prison a certain amount which amounts to be about only like nine dollars. But that's a lot of money in here."

The fact that the average laborers making the tourist knickknacks in the prison earn only about forty cents an hour provides an indication of just how valuable nine dollars is inside the walls. The guards take other cuts besides the nine dollars a month and the surcharge on raw materials. "Whenever the guards want to eat," Phil easily understands, "I can't really say no. I end up paying about five different times for everything. So what that means is that my prices have to be so high that the real people who suffer in here are the people with no money." For those without money, it's the beans and rice line.

Phil offers me one of his hamburgers as his guest. The usual price is just over a dollar. "In here that's a lot of money, when you're only making less than forty cents an hour."

So how do his customers get that kind of cash? Easy, explains this jailhouse economist. "They help the guards bring in drugs for them to sell in here. They work and they only eat once a day. They sell everything they've got on the outside and their wives bring them the money in here. The way we sum it up is: The United States prisons, they're harder on the prisoners. Down here it's harder on the families."

For Phil, the experience of not knowing when his case will be adjudicated, when he will be released, creates a feeling of stagnation. He says he's becoming more and more bitter. "Mexico is a very rich country, with very poor people and a very crooked government," he counsels. "Never come down here alone. That was my first mistake. If you've got money, don't let anybody know it; that's the second mistake. Make sure you've got insurance, or take a taxi."

He's offering sage advice about insurance and taxis. In 1991, sixty-four Americans were arrested in Mexico for traffic violations. It's enough of a problem to rate a boldface warning in the 1991 American Automobile Association guidebook to Mexico. "To understand what happens when an accident occurs in Mexico," cautions the guide, "you must realize that unlike most U.S. and Canadian law, Mexican law is based on the Napoleonic Code, which presumes guilt until innocence is proven.

Thus, all parties involved in an accident are detained for assessing responsibility."

Don't worry too much about fender benders, states the guide. "But if the accident causes injury or death, the operators will be jailed until the authorities determine who is at fault. Then only the responsible driver will remain incarcerated until he or she guarantees restitution to the victims and payment of the fine imposed for causing the accident."

Too many Americans don't realize that an automobile accident is a criminal offense in Mexico. Most Americans don't know that buying a valid insurance policy does not prevent a driver from being jailed after involvement in an accident.

Especially since the release of the movie *Midnight Express,* most people believe that the majority of Americans locked up overseas are behind bars because they ran afoul of some country's harsh drug laws. That's not the case. At any given time at least a few thousand Americans are behind bars far from home, and most of them are imprisoned for offenses other than drug charges, such as immigration law violations, being drunk and disorderly, fraud, and theft. Marijuana is by far the drug most likely to be involved in American violations of foreign drug laws, and these occur most often in Mexico, the Bahamas, or Jamaica.

Americans jailed overseas fall into two categories, which simplistically and conveniently can be called good guys and bad guys. The bad guys were caught knowingly committing a crime, an act illegal at home and abroad. The goods guys are, at worst, naive. They did something that was legal at home, but illegal where they did it. And some are completely innocent of any wrongdoing.

Illinois businessman Richard Flynn was one of the good guys. He went to Mexico to negotiate a solution to a business dispute between the company he worked for in Chicago and a Mexican firm. Once Flynn was south of the border and within the jurisdiction of the Mexican judicial system, the Mexican company's representatives charged the American with illegal business practices. Flynn was arrested and thrown in jail.

Three years and three heart attacks later, the battered businessman was finally released from custody and headed home. His case had worked its way up to the Mexican Supreme Court. While he whiled away the years, becoming sicker and receiving inadequate medical care, his conviction was reversed and he was completely exonerated of any criminal behavior.

Unlike Carol, Alex, and Phil, whose prior problems and lifestyles might suggest to overworked U.S. consular officials that their cases deserved a low priority, Richard Flynn was a middle-class, all-American businessman. But he, too, came home feeling let down by his government. There is a pattern to such disappointment. Few Americans who run afoul of foreign legal systems come home convinced the U.S. government did all it could to help them out of their difficulties.

Like so many victims of foreign jurisprudence, Richard's wife, Catherine, who commuted between Chicago and Mexico City working to win her husband's release, was amazed at how little assistance they received during the ordeal from the U.S. government. "I think that the State Department has done what they could do," she said carefully just after the announcement that Richard was being released. "Obviously I was always disappointed that not everything I felt could have been done was done. But I guess that's a difference of perceptions."

The Flynns, in fact, sued the State Department because it refused to allow one of its consular officers to testify at Richard's Mexican trial. The Flynns wanted the testimony because the officer was a witness to the disputed contract negotiations, a witness the Flynns were sure would convince the Mexican authorities that Richard was acting in good faith to correct the contract dispute between the American and Mexican companies. The State Department claimed international treaties and diplomatic policies prevented the consular officer from being a witness. So Richard was convicted of fraud and drew a six-year sentence along with a fine of one and one-half million dollars.

"We all have this view that because we're Americans, if we go to a foreign country and get in trouble our embassy will automatically help us," Catherine Flynn reflected on her family's trauma. "During this three-year ordeal, I found that that's not really the case. It's very limited really, what they do."

What the U.S. government does to help American citizens in trouble abroad is indeed often very limited. What isn't so limited is what the U.S. government can do to help, if it chooses to provide assistance. It is extraordinarily disturbing to learn just how duplicitous and how politically motivated are the decisions whether to extend such help. In addition to the geopolitical considerations of the State Department and the White House, the fate of Americans in prison in other countries often depends on the interest, expertise, and whimsy of consular officers on duty.

Languishing in Lima,
Tears in Annapolis

Although certain illegal drugs are readily available, anyone carrying any is almost automatically assumed to be a drug trafficker. If arrested on any charge the wait for trial in prison can take a year and is particularly unpleasant.

> Warning for travelers in Peru from
> the *South American Handbook*

El Sexto Prison is one of the greater toilets of the world. It makes *Midnight Express* look like Sunnybrook Farm.

> American lawyer Robert Fogelnest,
> a specialist in Peruvian cases

|||||||||||||||||||| **M**y vivid memory of Winnie Rincon is listening to her tales of horror as the birds cheerfully chirp in her Annapolis, Maryland, suburban back yard. The sad stories competing with those soft birdsongs reflect the cultural contrasts and moral crises that assaulted her for years following her son's arrest in Peru.

"It needs to be talked about because people just don't realize." She starts to tell her family's story of terror and heartbreak. "They're left," she says, referring to her son Chris and all the other Americans rotting in the prisons of Peru. "To me, it is like a big spider and they're in this huge web and the spider plays with them and they either will die or they will survive."

There was no question about Chris's guilt or innocence. He was caught breaking the law, trying to smuggle *pasta* out of Peru, the raw coca paste that is refined into cocaine in the final chemical process of making the drug from the coca plant. Possession of *pasta* is not just illegal in Peru, it is illegal in the United States too, and transporting two hundred grams of the narcotic is drug trafficking by anyone's definition. Chris Rincon was one of the bad guys: in his early twenties, not too sophisticated, not well educated, traveling through South America trying to make some quick and illegal money.

"It's my son," Winnie tells me in her back yard as she tries to reconcile the fact that she is working to get Chris out of prison in Peru despite the fact that she considers drug trafficking a heinous crime that should be harshly punished. "He made a mistake. He's a young boy, and he made a mistake."

I speak with her gently, she seems so on edge. But I want to know why she feels so strongly that Chris and the other Americans in jail should be helped if she wants drug trafficking stopped. Why shouldn't society, I ask her, just leave her son in prison?

"Because we're human beings and we just don't do that with another human being. I don't see how anyone can just lock you up and throw away the key; that's just not done, to my way of thinking."

It is a difficult conversation for her, but something she has clearly thought through. This middle-class, conservative, law-abiding American mother is being forced through the actions of her black-sheep offspring to reconsider philosophies that she has accepted most of her adult life.

"In our prison system, sometimes we do too much for the prisoners," she reflects about what she sees as policies soft on crime and criminals at home. "But at the same time, you have to give them the basics. You have to give them three meals a day, at least." She forces a laugh and changes that, "two meals a day, at least. Down in Peru they were lucky if they got their *paella*. It was rice, I saw it. It was brought in oil drums, they were cut in half, and the rice was just piled in there. It was put outside the prison on the road. Then they had milk cans of a sort of type of soup, to me it looked like corn and potatoes mixed together. But the flies, the flies just covered all that rice." She manages another laugh. "And to think that someone has to eat that, that they have to survive on that with the dirt from the roads and everything. And then when it's brought into the prison, it's just put there and the prisoners just fight. It isn't doled out, here this is yours and that's yours. It's just plunked there and the prisoners fight over it. I sat there in this little courtyard.

My son said, 'It's time that they're going to serve *paella*, let's go out.' He went, bought a bench from someone."

The words are now pouring out as Winnie Rincon relives her nightmare visit to Peru. She remembers her sudden introduction into the twisted world of tough Latin American prisons, of a normal American life gone awry because of a stupid criminal mistake. She realizes that even the terminology needs explanation, strange ideas like "buying" a bench. Prisoners and their visitors must pay guards or other prisoners who have accumulated power and property for even a place to sit.

"We went out in the courtyard." As we talk, she's drifting back to the disturbing scene she witnessed of food being served to indigent prisoners; it was an initiation into her son's brutal daily prison environment. "We were sitting here, naturally talking with the other Americans and everything. All of a sudden I really wanted to get up and leave." Her voice cracks with strain from the memory. "I didn't know what was happening. I was scared. One of the Americans laughed and he said, 'Mrs. Rincon, what's the matter?' I said, 'What is going on?' It was as if they were going to start a big, huge fight and they were going to kill each other. And that's an everyday occurrence."

Winnie Rincon brought lunch that day to the prison, chicken for Chris and his friends. "There was a young Canadian boy and he was standing with his bowl behind his back. I was watching him and saying, 'He does not want to go up there and get that; it's a disgrace to him to have to go up there and fight for his survival. But he knows that if he doesn't he has no chance to live.' I was thinking to myself, why doesn't my son offer him the chicken? But I thought, you know, I'm not going to get involved with the prison rules, because there are rules for the prison and you just don't get involved. But just as I was thinking that to myself, my son said, 'Richard, never mind about getting your *paella* today, my mother brought some chicken.' So that's what he did."

Winnie sighs a mother's sigh. Then she remembers another domestic encounter with her son's friends and their netherworld. Back inside one of the prison buildings, "I sat back on the couch, but, oh, I sat up real quick because it's filthy." She switches back and forth between the past and present tenses as she tells the story. The memories are so intense she seems to be back inside the prison walls in Peru as she recounts the experiences, not in her own placid Annapolis neighborhood. "It's dirty. I thought, oh my goodness, I'm going to get bugs, I'm going to get something. Richard said, 'What's the matter, Mrs. Rincon?' I said, 'Oh, I just realized it's dirty, that I don't want to lean back.' He said, 'Oh, no, no, no, this is clean, this is clean!' I thought he was kidding me and I said, 'Yeah, Richard, sure it's clean.' He said, 'No, really, Mrs. Rincon, this is my bed, it's clean.' And I felt terrible, because it was filthy, it was bad. But I leaned back."

She sighs again. "No one can believe, it has to happen to you to understand. It's just inhumane how they treat you. Maybe I'm wrong, but I really think the families suffer more than the prisoners. The prisoners, yes they do suffer very much, don't get me wrong. But with us, we try so hard to do something, and there's nothing we can do. There are really very few things that you can do. You want to say, 'Why can't you get them out of there?' But, no, it's just not possible."

Winnie Rincon's nightmare started with a telephone call from the State Department. "I felt like stone. I was dead inside. It was numbness. I just couldn't believe." She starts to sob for a moment reliving the call, and then remembers her next emotion. "You get mad, you get very mad." The sob turns to a sharp little laugh. "I got mad and I thought, oh, I'd just like to take him and shake him good. I felt he was lost, that we'd be lucky if we ever got him back."

Winnie made the trip down to Washington the next day and began what became for her a productive relationship with the State Department and its Emergency Overseas Citizens Center. "You understand that they can just do so much. Yes, I'd like them to do a lot more. I don't know all the ins and outs of what they are supposed to do and what they're not supposed to do, but I do feel they were very helpful. I'm satisfied with what they did with our family."

Winnie wrestles with her feelings and her politics. Yes, she feels satisfied with the work the State Department did for her family, but on a more abstract level, she wishes that the U.S. government would exert more pressure against foreign governments that hold Americans in their miserable prisons. She recognizes that, perversely, the Peruvian style of vicious justice is sometimes successful, that it may well have scared her son out of a life of crime and addiction. She also is aware the U.S. government officially encourages drug-filled nations like Peru to get tough with cocaine manufacturers and traffickers. Parents like Winnie, the prisoners, and human rights activists want that same U.S. government to interfere with the draconian judicial processes in these drug-producing countries, corrupt processes that too often result in ludicrously long prison sentences for small-time dealers.

"The whole system in Peru – in foreign countries – is usually a sham," is her irritated reflection. One of her favorite examples is the telephone calls she received from Chris. The State Department had told her it was impossible for the two of them to talk over the phone. So whenever she got a call from Chris, a call he could arrange with a ten-dollar bribe, she would immediately tell the State Department about the communication. And they would respond by simply telling her that such a call was not possible, that the Peruvian authorities would not allow such a thing. "It's all a sham," she says again.

Winnie is convinced that while Chris's experience may well set his life straight, it did nothing to ameliorate America's drug problem. "It's a laugh, because all they're arresting is the little kid off the corner, usually. It's usually just the kid that wants to bring the drug back, a lot of times for their own use. They don't arrest the big person. Nobody who is really involved in bringing drugs in a large quantity into the United States is ever arrested and put into jail."

She feels too removed from policy-making to understand the answer to this dilemma; she worries that she doesn't enjoy access to enough information to really know what the best solution might be. "Why I say the State Department and the embassy helped me is because every time I wrote to them, they answered my letters. They would even call me from the embassy and tell me things."

The U.S. government, for example, warned her about dishonest lawyers trying to taking advantage of still another relatively affluent family in distress, like the smooth-talking lawyer on the long-distance phone line who offered to help Chris in return for an advance commission of twenty thousand dollars. By the time Chris returned to the United States, the family investment in his care, feeding, and legal fees topped thirty thousand dollars, but it was money that the family felt was spent legitimately.

"It was killing me." She sounds pained as she explains how she and her husband drew the line on how much they would spend on Chris's defense. They decided to use their life savings to work for his release, but not sell their house in Annapolis. "Day in and day out it was killing me, knowing that my son was down there. Knowing that he might become a drug addict down in there and that if he ever did come back, say in five to ten years, that he wouldn't be a human. He would be something . . . ." Her voice trails off.

She started writing to Chris, and sent a letter south every day until he was released. "Just anything, about his brothers, about what I did during the day. You need letters when you are away from your family. You need to have something to know that somebody's there. When you're away from your family, you feel nobody knows me, nobody cares."

Letters came back from Chris. They tell two stories: they provide intimate details of the sordid conditions for Americans in Latin American prisons and they offer a penetrating glimpse into the changes in Chris Rincon's character—both the deterioration and the growth—as the months slipped by.

The first letters try to present a calming picture under the circumstances.

First of all I want to let you know I'm alive and well. So far I haven't had any problems with any of the other prisoners and I don't think I will, because they are usually interested in talking to an American to find out what life in the United States is like. The prison guards are worse criminals than the prisoners themselves, because they take everything they can from you whether you like it or not. For example, I had to pay the guards ten dollars to sleep here, where I am in a cell by myself. I also get to take a shower tomorrow morning.

I haven't written to you yet because it's very difficult to do anything because they lock you up and that's that. Also I've been moved to two different places so far. It makes you think a lot when you know you're going some place else, but you don't know when, where, or how.

The first place I went after my arrest at the airport was to the police holding cell where they do the first step in my paperwork. I was there 19 days and they don't let you have a pen there. Now I'm at (so far eight days) step two, a holding cell under the judge's office. I found myself complaining about the first place which wasn't so bad, now that I'm here and see how bad it can really be.

I think it might be helpful to me if you could send me some info on how the law system works down here in Peru. They arrested me with 200 grams of pasta, so anything you can send would be helpful to me. Since I'm here and in the situation I'm in, there is nothing much I can do about it.

When I'm in prison and settled in I will write more often.

Debby Elliot* has been very helpful to me and I thank God for her because if it weren't for her I wouldn't have any visitors. It makes me feel real good knowing that she will be visiting me once a week.

I want you to know I love you, Dad, and the whole family very much, much more than you realize, even more than I realized. Since I've been down here I find myself thinking about you all and wondering if everyone is okay, because we all have our problems, but hopefully none of you have a problem you can't solve. I look at the picture of the family you sent me every day, remembering when we were all together.

Just a few days later he wrote from El Sexto Prison, again filling the letter with details about his squalid new lifestyle. "I know I let you all down and I'm making a lot of unneeded trouble for you," he apologized, and then started philosophizing.

How was your Fourth of July? Did the fireworks go off for you? The Fourth of July was my first day in prison. Ironic isn't it. You know, the Fourth of July never meant more to me than a day off and a night to drink, now that I've lost my freedom I really see the Fourth of July for what it really means. After being here for the short time I have, it seems I was living my life in black and white and when I get out it will be in full color. People don't seem to appreciate something until they don't have it anymore.

You can't imagine how dirty it is here. I worry about my health. It's really very crowded here. All the foreigners stay in a separate place at night. It's a restaurant and I use the term loosely, and I sleep on the floor with other people. It's not very clean, but that's the way things go here. I'm still healthy both mentally and physically. I pray to God to help me stay that way.

Don't think I'm not writing; it's just hard to get paper or should

---

* Debby Elliot was the U.S. consular officer assigned to the Chris Rincon case when he was arrested in Lima. She corresponded with the elder Rincons about the case until she was reassigned to Washington, and she received high marks from the family for her productive involvement in their case. In one letter she reassured the Rincons about the sixty dollars a month Chris was spending in prison, "I don't think Chris is paying for friendship, but he is paying for avoiding the creation of enemies." She told them prior to their visit to El Sexto, "After these months of communication, I feel like a distant member of the family."

I say it's hard to do anything here. Well, I don't have much paper, so I will write you again soon because I sure have a lot of time on my hands. I have to get a routine down so I don't just sleep, eat and think about how to get out. It's easy to lose your mind here.

A month later the letters were filling up with that prison routine, stories of fights between prisoners and shakedowns of the convicts and their cells by the corrupt guards. "The police," wrote Chris, "from the moment I was arrested till even now have robbed, lied to me, and beat me." It wasn't a bad beating, he reassured his family, just one designed to scare him. And he was clearly spending a lot of contemplative time.

There is really no one to sit down with and just talk with. At least no one that is in the same frame of mind as I am. You seem to have friends here as long as you have money. I guess you find out who is really your friend when you no longer have money. I hope I don't have that same problem. I try to find the good in everything and everyone I come in contact with. When I give I want to give without the expectation of receiving anything in return, as it says in the Bible. But I also wonder if it's my true feeling or if it's just that I have read it in the Bible. What are feelings, thoughts or emotion? I think adaptation is the key to survival.

More than a month later, Chris apologizes for not writing, "but I have been getting lazy or maybe not lazy but I am letting this place get to me." He complains that every day is the same and that the routine is wearing him down.

Like this morning, I was carrying a bucket of water for my shower to the bathroom and as I was walking to the bathroom someone spit in it. And things like this always happen and it can shorten your temper after a whole day of little mishaps.

The soap you sent me for fungus is great. If you can try and send me some at least once a month, it might help keep some of the fungus off me.

If it's not too much trouble for you I would enjoy getting the Baltimore newspaper to read. I have something to ask which I think Dad can help me with and that is to send me a pair of work gloves so I can walk on my hands and do my exercises because I refuse to put my hands on the ground here since people piss and spit all over.

Well, I am getting used to seeing the rats run around all the time. I think I will start naming them for something else to do. As far as my lawyers go, I haven't seen them since the last time they came. They were supposed to see me last Wednesday so I think I will call them today or tomorrow and see what is happening. Being locked up and losing your freedom makes us all see things, life, differently. Sometimes I want to hit anything near me when I think about this. It hurts me, but it's a hurt you can't do anything about.

By the time Chris marked a half year locked up in Peru, the letters started rambling more, and he knew it. "I have in the last month been going through a real confused state of emotions," he wrote. "I don't want you to think I am going crazy. George, the one-armed guy from Africa, was caught doing what he shouldn't have and if you don't make the guards happy you will have trouble." He told of tightened security after two Americans and a Peruvian escaped; he worried about losing his telephone opportunities.

The next day he wrote again. "I slept most of the day. Cellmates despise me because I don't give them money. Things I write make no sense to you." A few days later he started to dream of a visit from his parents. "Be prepared to see, smell, and hear some very unpleasant things," he cautioned, "but don't let these things worry you because I think I have got it under control."

Thanksgiving passed, Christmas, the New Year. "Lately I try real hard at night to listen to noises from the street. In the morning when I wake up and climb the wall to exercise I always look at one tree that I can see from the top of the wall. It really is a pretty sight."

After another month, another slice of prison life. "I did lose my temper today. One rat stole my towel, but my bodyguard got it back. I thought it was funny, so the rat then took some trash and threw it on me while I was all soaped up. I walked out after him and began punching him. This is how my day began."

The letters continue, day after day, filled with a stream of metaphysical questions and thoughts. After a year, he wrote: "So far I am pretty proud of myself because there are all kinds of drugs to do or get in here, but I am doing good at staying away from them because this place gets to you and sometimes you just want to escape the situation. Anyway, you

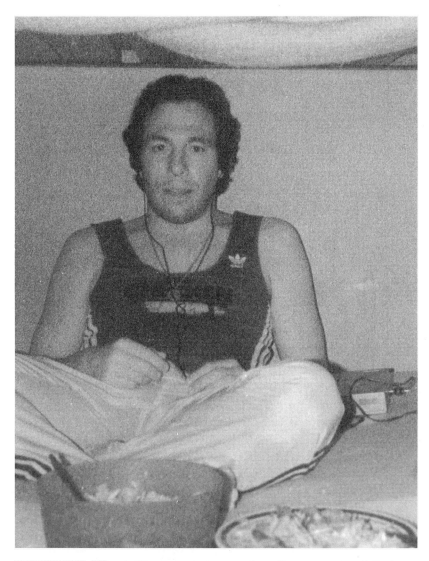

||||||||||||||||||||||| **W**innie Rincon took this snapshot of her son in Lima's El Sexto Prison and smuggled it out of Peru. About her photographs, she writes, "They really *do not* show the horror of the place. The smell is still with me. A horse stable that is never cleaned." (Photo: Winnie Rincon)

can't, but don't worry, I am keeping away from the wrong things. Even though today we got hold of a few drinks on this night."

A few days later, Chris reported, "Tarzan lent me his TV; Jose and I watched Jimmy Swaggert." After Swaggert they watched a documentary about prison life in Peru. "They even told of a guy in prison two years and found innocent. So they know the problems, but I don't understand why they don't do something about it."

In another letter Chris relays home the news that Richard might be going crazy. "The embassy came today. Brought our vitamins and the nurse came also and gave us a hepatitis shot. When I first got here and the first time I saw the nurse, she didn't turn me on or I didn't think she was beautiful, just a nice woman. But as time goes on and I am in here longer, she gets better looking every time I see her and today I thought she was the most beautiful woman. It just shows me that I am changing."

Finally, well over a year after his arrest at the Lima airport, Chris Rincon's day in court came.

Woke early and went to shower and got dressed for court. Yanyez let me use some of his clothes since he is about my same size. Pablo and Frenchy also are going to court today. When you go to court you get fingerprinted and they put a stamp on your arm. Then when they call your name you go out the second door, out front and the guards search you, then handcuff you to another person, then you squat down. But Pablo and I paid the guards not to handcuff us and not to push us around.

Then you run out the front door to the bus with the guards on both sides of you. You take a seat on the bus with the guards on both sides of you. It's about a twenty-minute drive to the courthouse. When you get to the courthouse you also pay to get in a clean cell with clean people. Then I sat there all day till four o'clock when they took me to see the judge.

When I got to the courtroom I was very nervous because it's a big empty room with a bench for me to sit on and a large desk with one big chair in the middle where the President sits and two smaller chairs for the other two judges, one on each side of the President. When you first look at them they look like three Gods ready to judge you. Each wearing a red ribbon with some type of gold medal hanging from the neck. I almost had to laugh because it's so primitive [compared] to our type of court system we know in the States. The first thing they told me is they think I deserve ten years and a ten-thousand-dollar fine. So it makes you wonder why you are there. I can't talk to my lawyer unless the judge says I can and my lawyer is sitting on my right, but not next to me. He is on the far right of the room and on my left is the State Attorney. I sit on a big bench in the middle of the room facing the three Gods, no jury, only three judges. Well, I was up there for about fifteen minutes.

Chris Rincon did draw the recommended sentence. Finally, well over two years after he was first caught with the *pasta*, Rincon headed back to the airport and home to America, but not freedom. I caught up with him at the federal penitentiary in Atlanta. Finally eligible for release from Peru under the terms of the prisoner transfer treaty in effect between the United States and Peru, Chris was serving out his time in relative comfort.

The high concrete walls at Atlanta, the guard towers, the double rows of chain-link fencing topped with barbed wire, the barred windows, all make the prison look imposing and threatening. Prisoners are yelling back and forth through their windows at each other; they're yelling down to the street to their girlfriends coming to visit. Tough as Atlanta looks and is, to Rincon it is a resort hotel.

"I'm glad to be back here," he tells me right away.

The words tumble out, the sentences often incomplete, as he describes the miserable conditions of Peruvian prison life. "Everything is wrong in there. The guards bring in drugs, weapons, sell that to people, whiskey, whatever you wanted in there, you could get. And more. All you had to do was pay." Chris pauses to make sure his message is adequately conveyed. From the controlled environment of the Atlanta Penitentiary, it seems a long reach even for him to fully understand the life he has just experienced. "You could pay to escape. I could've escaped, but I needed, say, eight thousand dollars. And I couldn't get that from anybody; nobody would come and say, 'Here's eight thousand, go escape.' Which was the problem."

But despite the market-driven economy of the Peruvian prison, it was nothing like the relative comfort and security of Mexico's La Mesa. Chris draws a picture of an overcrowded prison, filthy and rife with disease caused by the dirt and the foul drinking water, filled not only with unfortunates and criminals, but barely tolerable misery. He tells about beatings from the guards during the shakedowns, in which cells were looted of television sets, electric fans, anything that was not carried out of the cells by the prisoners. "It was bad. We always had to have one person watching the room or they would come in and steal everything," he says about the living quarters that provided him with some protection from his fellow inmates. "In a small cell, I'd say it was ten by five, something like that, there were seven of us. There were four beds and on one of the beds there were two guys, so right there there were five people. And there was one guy on the floor between the two beds and another guy. Now these guys that slept on the floor usually cleaned our dishes, cleaned the floor, things like that, so they'd have a spot. That's how they paid for that spot to sleep. Because if they didn't sleep there we could kick them out and they'd have to sleep outside, unless somebody else took them in to wash dishes. Now a lot of guys became faggots, or whatever, to get places like that." He is trying not to sound judgmental. "They did what they had to do to survive, okay? Luckily I didn't. My family supported me a hundred percent. I came out of there just like I went over, you know. I didn't lose anything because I spent a lot of money. I spent the money for people to leave me alone."

Chris Rincon relates one outrageous story of abuse after another, until he stumbles on one memory that makes him laugh. "I remember one incident when I was in the restaurant there. Like we have bouncers in a bar to keep the rowdy people out, they had a bouncer for this restaurant to keep the guys that were hungry out, the guys that would come and bother you. The foreigners would go in there and sit down and eat a plate; the other people would come in and try to take things from us, or steal things from us when we weren't looking. In order to make the restaurant more appealing to the foreigners, they had this bouncer to keep the other people out, okay? I remember I was eating a meal one time, and this one black guy came in, a Peruvian, and he was asking me for food or something and the bouncer said, 'Get out, you gotta get out.' And the guy wasn't listening to him. So all of a sudden this bouncer took the fork out of my hand and stabbed the guy, you know. And then gave me back my fork. I looked around to see if anybody was awed at what happened. But it was just like a normal incident." Chris smiles.

"I was, hey, give me another fork at least. That's when I realized why they had this bouncer." He laughs again, a pained snigger. The guard knocks, our visit is over.

Some of the desperate foreigners Chris left behind in Peru used him as a conduit for their cries for help. "We need pressure on Peru to get foreigners sentenced," Allan Walden wrote to Chris. "We are isolated, as usual, here, with few outside contacts, but we're persevering, trying to get our story out to the world. We need pressure on Peru to get foreigners sentenced." Americans cannot take advantage of the transfer treaty between Peru and the United States until they have been convicted of a crime, sentenced to prison for it, and served part of the term.

One petition sent to Chris from Luringancho Prison in Lima pleaded, "There are many European, American, and Canadian tourists in Luringancho Prison, some falsely accused, others with small amounts, of being 'drug traffickers.' Many of them were arrested by police officials who collude with 'lawyers' in what is actually an extortion racket. The victims of these extortions suffer for years in prison waiting for trial, while the same officials who arrested them perversely participate in voluminous drug trafficking." Those who signed wrote their names and the status of their cases.

Gerard S. Baril, for example, listed himself as enduring twenty-two months in Luringancho without the benefit of a trial. For David R. Sickles, the figure was twenty-seven months, again with no trial. Two of their comrades from Germany described themselves as Luringancho inmates for almost four years without a court conviction.

In another letter, the inmates write, "Many of us have been set up by police officials that themselves are heavily involved in drug trafficking, that have tortured us, stolen our personal belongings, and work together with a group of 'lawyers' to extort sums of over U.S. $20,000 – in some cases for the allegedly necessary payments of bribes."

The letter warns, "Lima has become one of the most dangerous places in the world for a foreign visitor because he could find himself in a situation where he may have to face an ordeal of five, ten or more years in a prison of Dante-esque conditions in the desert."

The inmates ask the world press and human rights organizations to come to Lima and witness the "cruel circumstances" in Peruvian prisons. They call for the establishment of some sort of international commission to study their cases to learn why "it is little wonder when many of us leave this place after many years as drug addicts, sick, undernourished, desocialized and sometimes even insane."

One of the lasting lessons for Chris is a civics warning. "Most of us are very ignorant," he preaches now. "You go to this other country, right there you've lost your rights as an American citizen. You don't have it, it's not the same. You know, I'm over there and here they are arresting me and I feel like saying, 'Hey, you can't do this to me!' But they don't want to hear that. I was locked up and that was it."

His mother hears a different message. "Our society has to put all these drugs behind us," is Winnie Rincon's conclusion from her nightmare. "The society has to finally realize that drugs are ruining our country."

Help from Home

In the very beginning, the government tried to
shut up all of the hostage families and told us if
we remained quiet they would get the hostages out
quicker. Well, we gave them a whole year and they
did nothing. So Peggy [Say] started a campaign and
all across the country those of us involved cam-
paigned for the release of the hostages. All the ex-
hostages have told us that without the publicity,
those men, they all would have been shot a long
time ago because if they were so devalued – you
know – if we paid no attention to the hostages, they
would be devalued in their eyes, so there was no
need to keep them alive. So the hostages' families
have been on the fence for a long, long time not
knowing when to shut up and when to keep talking.

> Rusty Ruth, a spokesperson for the U.S.
> hostages held in Lebanon, in a conversation
> with the author on December 3, 1991, as her
> cousin Terry Anderson was being released

|||||||||||||||||||| There is an obvious distinction between the Americans
locked up in foreign countries as a consequence of an official judicial
process and those Americans who, over the past several years, have been
victims of free-lance hostage takers. The prisoners of government-
sanctioned arrests and court proceedings face a different set of problems
and options than do hostages, but they often share a common complaint:
frustration with the efforts conducted on their behalf by their own
government.

Jesse Jackson responded to that dissatisfaction during his 1984
presidential campaign. He returned from a visit to Fidel Castro with

twenty-two American citizens in tow. The Americans had all been arrested in Cuba or Cuban territorial waters and charged with illegal drug trafficking or drug possession. For the former prisoners, Jackson's personal diplomacy achieved what the U.S. government chose not to, or couldn't, achieve: their freedom. Castro got rid of twenty-two undesirable aliens and scored some propaganda points against the Reagan administration; Jackson enjoyed publicity for his candidacy.

Elbert Cheatham had been in Cuban jails for about a year, charged with possessing seventeen hundred pounds of marijuana. He called to reporters, as he headed home to Lynchburg, Virginia, fresh from Jackson's airlift to Dulles Airport, "Tell Jackson thanks a million! Jesse Jackson is Jesus Christ right now." Another returning prisoner, Mark McDermott, spent two years in Castro's prisons. He was arrested when his boat approached the Cuban coast and charged with drug trafficking, a crime he denied at Dulles. "They gave us a choice between pleading guilty to smuggling marijuana or spying," he told waiting reporters, "and we were advised that they shot spies."

There were other Americans in Cuba whom Jackson couldn't release, or who didn't want to leave because they would face criminal charges back in the United States. About sixty airplane hijackers were in Cuba when that crime was in vogue. Many were kept not in a prison, but in a special home provided by the Cuban government for American hijackers. Only a few are still on the island.

Before the Berlin Wall fell in 1989, there were few Americans locked up in so-called Communist countries. Usually when Americans were caught and charged with crimes—whether political or criminal, committed intentionally or by mistake—they were simply expelled from the country. That's what East Germany did repeatedly with an Oregon man who periodically climbed up on the top of the Wall with a pickax. As a personal protest against the barrier, he would swing his ax high and chop into the concrete. Usually he would manage to chip out a few chunks before he was hauled off by the *Grenzpolizei*, questioned, and deported. When East Germany unified with West Germany, as far as the State Department knew, there were no Americans waiting in East German prisons.

One reason for the lack of problems with authorities in Communist countries may well be that Americans traveling in regions of the world governed by the Communists were more careful and restrained than those traveling in freer societies. A few generations of anti-Communist propaganda by the American government likely convinced many Americans that Communist police states were not good places to take chances.

An exception was a case that some newspapers called "the Moscow connection." Three bungling smugglers committed one of the most serious crimes ever charged to Americans in the Soviet Union when they landed at Sheremetyevo Airport with sixty-two pounds of heroin. The trio never thought that Soviet customs agents would inspect their luggage at Sheremetyevo, because they were just transit passengers, changing planes on their way from Kuala Lumpur, where they bought the drugs, to Amsterdam, where they planned to get rich selling them. But their false-bottom suitcases didn't fool the inspectors.

The three were sent to a special labor camp for foreigners in Mordovia, east of Moscow. One of the smugglers described it to the *Washington Post* when he finally returned to the United States as "a village, really a shantytown. Ever been to Laredo? On the Texas-Mexican border? Dilapidated little structures, horses and wagons. It was like the world ended there." He said he was up at six, sent outside to exercise, then was served "fish soup, just water with some fish boiled in it, the worst thing to smell at six in the morning. I always gave it a pass." He worked all day and was subjected to political lectures in the evening. "They'd show you a picture, people lying in the street. They'd say, 'They got 40,000 people without homes in New York.' I'd say, 'Hey, gimme New York.' "

Some Americans traveling in Communist countries suffered encounters with police that started as traffic violations or auto accidents. They spent a few nights in jail while the paperwork was sorted out and then were deported. Typical American arrogance toward authority and unfamiliarity with the tradition of paying cash for tickets on the spot contributed to whatever problems Americans faced on Communist highways.

Back in the early eighties, I was stopped along the transit road through East Germany to Berlin. In those days, driving from West Germany to West Berlin meant taking one of only three available routes. A special transit visa was issued by the East German government allowing no deviation from the specified routes. There was no speed limit on the West German autobahns; speed was restricted to a maximum of one hundred kilometers per hour on the East German roads to Berlin.

I came around one curve to find a quick series of temporary signs reducing the legal speed from one hundred to eighty to sixty kilometers per hour in just a few hundred yards. I sailed on at about a hundred and was quickly pulled over by a *Volkspolizei* who suddenly appeared, waving alongside the road. I learned later that these speed traps were almost always set up on the transit roads, and that the police watched for Western license plates. It was a method of earning hard currency for the cash-strapped East German government.

But I was new to Germany then and annoyed by the setup. After I got out of the car, my passport was taken along with my driver's license, and I was ordered to pay an eighty-mark cash fine on the spot. I refused and started arguing with the policeman. As he repeatedly demanded the cash, I glared at him. I spoke no German at the time, and he spoke no English. We worked with sign language, a few cognates that we quickly found, and mutual disgust and disrespect. It was a perfect recipe for trouble—for me.

As he insisted on the money, he held all the cards, specifically my passport and driver's license. My car was pulled over, and my wife and infant son held along with all my baggage. He was armed, backed up by authority and several other policemen. Instead of looking for the most expeditious avenue out of this unfortunate but not too serious situation, I made matters worse. I started yelling at him, explaining in English that he couldn't understand how unreasonable his speed trap was because the change in speed limit was sudden and unannounced. He didn't know the precise meaning of my words, so he may well have interpreted them to be worse than they were because my tone was so offensive. It was a moot argument anyway because he obviously knew how unfair the trap was.

Then I told him collecting cash was corrupt. Yelling and miming the moves of taking a drink, I told him, "You just want the eighty marks to buy beer!" That was a really stupid, counterproductive thing for me to do. He understood my meaning perfectly, and I was lucky that my wife defused the situation and quickly paid him. She just wanted to get away from him and get back on the road.

The next day when I recounted the experience to one of the diplomats at the U.S. embassy in East Berlin, he told me I had been a fool to argue and that my behavior was exactly the kind of action that landed Americans in jail in East Germany. He said we were really fortunate that my wife had offered the policeman the money, and that he had taken it. Probably the baby strapped in the backseat influenced his decision. But

my mistake was typical of the insensitive conduct that gets Americans
into difficulties away from home. I was acting like an American in
America, rather than a visitor to a foreign culture. I was not playing by
the local rules.

Certainly, young Jimmy Koros would agree with the assessment that
Communist legal systems are not worth crossing. By the beginning of
1992, after Communism and Gorbachev finally fell in the Soviet Union
and that empire collapsed, Jimmy was still in his cell, in the Kharkov
Pretrial and Transfer Prison in the Ukraine. He was hoping to get out
early if an appeals court overturned his conviction, but his two-year sentence was almost served.

I learned about the Koros case through the U.S. embassy in Moscow.
As far as the consular department there knew, while the Soviet Union
was breaking up, Koros was the only American prisoner serving time
anywhere in the former Soviet republics. Considering the huge land
mass that includes, it is astounding that more Americans were not
imprisoned there. Rumors and reports continued to circulate after *glasnost* that there were still American military prisoners of war from Vietnam, Korea, or even World War II locked up in Soviet camps, along
with some American civilians who were caught behind Red Army lines
after World War II. But Koros was the only American civilian on the
State Department books.

"They accuse him of being a kind of criminal," Koros's father Jerry
tells me in a thick Ukrainian accent over a scratchy telephone line from
Kharkov. I am calling from Moscow and we can barely hear one another.
"So far he's still alive, but he feels really bad."

Jerry is known in Kharkov by the name he used before the family
emigrated to America, Jennady Korostishevski. In 1977, the Korostishevski family, like so many other Soviet Jews, finally received their exit
visas and emigrated to New York. Jennady became Jerry Koros and his
young son Igor took the name Jimmy. Five years later, when Jerry and
his wife became naturalized American citizens, Jimmy was still under
eighteen. By American law, Jimmy automatically became a citizen, too.

On a typically frigid Moscow winter morning, I sit in the cozy apartment of William Englund, sipping coffee and listening to the tangled details of the Koros case. Englund, the Moscow bureau chief of the
Baltimore Sun, is just back from Kharkov. There he had pieced Jimmy's

sad story together, and managed to spend about an hour with him in the Pretrial and Transfer Prison warden's office, hearing his longing for his adopted homeland.

After the family moved to Brighton Beach, Jerry – a furrier by trade – worked as a cab driver, using whatever extra money he made to develop his new American fur business. Young Jimmy was busy becoming an American. He attended Sheepshead Bay High School, but by the time he was fifteen became more interested in a used Dodge Charger. He dropped out of school and spent much of his time at his father's shop, working on the hot rod.

Jerry did well with his taxi driving, but the fur business never fulfilled his dreams. Despite the relative affluence the family found in America, furs remain a luxury, and unlike in the Ukraine, the winter fur season in America is relatively short. Jerry blames those two factors for his fur business setbacks. As *glasnost* and *perestroika* came to the Soviet Union, he decided to return to the Ukraine and use his connections in both countries to prosper in the fur trade. He planned to make furs in the Ukraine, where costs were much lower, and then sell them in the United States.

Reporter Englund came away from his interviews with the impression that the fur business was not the only force driving the family back to Europe. Koros's wife missed the old country; their parents were getting old. For whatever combination of reasons, the family packed up in 1988 and made their way back to Kharkov, a typically dirty and crumbling Soviet city teeming with about a million people.

Their first brush with the Soviet law came as they went down to the *Ovir* office. *Ovir* is the government authority responsible for internal documents. All foreigners living in the Soviet Union were required to register with *Ovir*. There, the bureaucrats took the Koros's United States passports and issued them replacement Soviet passports. Jerry complained vociferously, but *Ovir* was adamant about its decision, saying the Koros family were Soviet citizens and the case was closed. Jerry called the U.S. embassy in Moscow and found out that *Ovir* had sent the family's passports there, apparently considering them American property. The U.S. authorities simply gave Jerry back the passports.

The Koros family business didn't prosper in the Ukraine either, but they lived well on their savings from America. Maybe too well. They built a two-story brick house in one of the best Kharkov neighborhoods and drove around in a shiny Mercedes. By Kharkov standards their lifestyle was ostentatious. But teenage Jimmy was miserable. He missed Brighton Beach, he missed his Dodge Charger. He missed America. Jimmy did make friends with another boy his age named Igor. This is where the intrigue starts. The other Igor was the son of one Nikolai Korsh, a former butcher who became a successful Kharkov business-man. Nikolai Korsh knew that in order to do business successfully in the changing Soviet society, it was necessary to cultivate friends in high places. Korsh's relationship with the deputy city prosecutor was an example of that networking. The prosecutor was influential in Kharkov society. He achieved some fame prosecuting dissidents during the Brezhnev years; the human rights organization Helsinki Watch identified the prosecutor as notorious then for fabricating cases. When he wasn't in the courtroom, this deputy prosecutor wrote detective stories. But among the shortages plaguing the Ukraine was a paper shortage. The prosecutor wanted to publish his mysteries. Businessman Nikolai Korsh made sure paper was available.

In January 1990, Korsh called the police and reported that his apartment had been burglarized. Lost, he said, were gold earrings, a gold ring and necklace, and some videotapes. Total value: about 9400 rubles.

Six months later, just past midnight on July 23, Jimmy Koros was hustled off the street into an unmarked car and asked, "What do you know about the burglary at the Korsh house?" He says the police in the car threatened him. "Get 45,000 rubles," he says he was told, "or you're going to be in lots of trouble." Jimmy wanted absolutely no trouble. His family had finally decided that Brighton Beach was a much better place than Kharkov. They were going back to their adopted homeland. Jimmy was ecstatic; he hated the Ukraine.

The next day, Jimmy made his way down to the police station. He says he felt he had nothing to fear because he knew nothing about the crime. He told the police that he knew nothing and that he didn't have 45,000 rubles for them. They arrested him.

By the Soviet law then in effect, police were obligated to charge him with some crime within three days or let him go. They kept Jimmy for thirty-four days without filing charges. During that time, says Jerry, Korsh approached him and suggested that all Jimmy's problems could be solved for 100,000 rubles. Jerry said his boy was innocent and there would be no deals.

Finally the police charged Jimmy with the burglary. They produced three boys as witnesses, who confessed to the actual break-in themselves, but identified Jimmy as the mastermind. He was tried in November. On the stand, all three of the boys retracted their confessions. There was no physical evidence linking Jimmy to any crime. He was found guilty of burglary and sentenced to four years.

The presiding judge was Alla Grigoreva. She's in her forties, a pleasant and smiling woman with a round face, highlighted by a touch of lipstick. At the time of the trial she was a Communist. "There wasn't any judge," she explains, "who wasn't a member of the Communist party." She quit abruptly in November 1990 when the new Ukrainian government advised all judges who wanted to keep their jobs to quit the party.

Englund talked with Judge Grigoreva, she was pleasant and cheerful. Why, he asked her, if the three witnesses recanted their confessions and there was no physical evidence against Jimmy, did she convict him? Her answer is a terrifying example of rationales for injustice. "The pretrial investigation pointed to his participation," she said about the confessions the police extracted from the three boys. "They couldn't explain the contradictions," she said about their decisions to renounce those confessions once they were in court, "so we found him guilty."

Jimmy, who all this time was held in prison, appealed the conviction. The appeals court looked at the record and ordered a retrial because Jimmy had not had a lawyer or a translator. Jimmy speaks Russian fluently, but he can't read or write it. He had been signing court papers when told to without knowing what they contained.

Jimmy sat in the Pretrial and Transfer Prison for a year waiting for the retrial. "They never acquit people right away here, the way they do in America," Judge Grigoreva explains about the long delay. But Jimmy wasn't acquitted after his second day in court, either. He was convicted again, and this time sentenced to two years by Judge Alexandr Shestak, who explained the lesser sentence, "He had already spent a long time in the pretrial prison—a year and a half—and conditions there are much worse than a prison camp."

After Jimmy's second trial, his father says Korsh offered to fix matters again. This time the price was 250,000 rubles and a car. Jerry Koros is convinced that Jimmy's problems are all the result of Korsh, with his connections in the police department and prosecutor's office, deciding that the rich Koros family was an easy mark for extortion.

The family refused to buy Jimmy's way out of prison, a decision Jimmy supports. Jimmy says he was approached in prison and told he could be released immediately if he'd drop his appeals and plead guilty.

|||||||||||||||||||||||| Young Jimmy Koros misses his Dodge Charger and the streets of Brooklyn from his cell in an old Ukrainian prison. (Photo: *Baltimore Sun* reporter Will Englund)

He refused. Instead he waits behind the massive gray walls and barbed wire of Kharkov's prison. He's housed in a cell with three other prisoners, furnished with four bunks and two chairs. He can watch television. Once a month his family can bring him sixteen pounds of food to supplement the meager prison diet. "It's slop," says Jimmy. "It's not fit for dogs or pigs." He's scrawny now, some sixty pounds lighter than when he was taken into custody.

Jimmy tries to stay out of trouble. He's been placed in solitary confinement twice, charged with insulting a guard. "I was beaten up more than once," he says. "They say, 'You talk too much.'" Apparently what he did to receive the beatings and removal to solitary was tell the guards he's an American citizen. In addition to the beatings, Jimmy says the guards threaten him with the rubber shirt. The rubber shirt is notorious among the prisoners at Kharkov. The guards pull it over the victim's head and then douse it with water. It shrinks, contracting against the chest, and breaking ribs.

In doublespeak that sounds like a parody of the Soviet stereotype, Kharkov Pretrial and Transfer Prison Chief Ivan Zanaziy refuses to accept responsibility for any wrong done to Jimmy by his guards. "We looked into that," he says about Jimmy's complaints, "and those facts don't confirm themselves."

"All I ever think about is Brooklyn," Jimmy says about his daily routine. He misses "normal life things. Fishing with my father, camping upstate, going to movies." He's outdoors only one hour a day, to exercise. "I try to keep far away from everyone. But talk you'll have to, or you'll go crazy." He worries about himself and his future. "You don't understand how you live here for a year and a half and slowly turn into an animal."

Englund appreciates Jimmy's concern. "The jailers were repulsive, sanctimonious people," he tells me as we discuss his visit with Jimmy. "They made me feel almost physically sick."

Russian human rights activist Andre Mironov took on Jimmy Koros's case. "I'm quite sure," he says, "he is not guilty at all. I think the reason is extortion; they tried to make his parents pay to release him. That is the only reason. There is no evidence against him." Mironov, who himself spent time in Soviet prison camps, says he's seen similar cases before. "This is a typical trait of the Soviet justice. When they start a case, they cannot turn back. Then they would be forced to admit that they made mistakes and it would have negative ramifications to their careers."

Jimmy's father tells me that just as soon as his son is out of prison,

"We go back to America. No question about it. If he'll be at home tomorrow, I'll go straight ahead to the airport." In the meantime, he sends Jimmy food—salami, milk, sugar—and spends his time and money doing everything he can think of to get his son out of prison. He's been allowed to visit a couple of times. They are separated by glass and can speak only over a telephone. "He can't give me any information," complains Jerry, "because somebody is listening." He's passed Jimmy some reading material, "the *New York Daily News* I find once and a William Shakespeare book."

Jimmy gets regular visits from American consular officers. They bring him vitamins and magazines. "I don't feel that much pressure," says Jerry about the U.S. embassy. "Maybe they are doing something. I don't get much information." Since Jimmy did not sign a Privacy Act waiver, the embassy will not discuss the case.

"I don't feel comfortable," sighs Jerry as we say good-bye. "They can make other problems for him. I don't trust them." His pessimism reminds me of a Russian joke about a prisoner: "He served all eight years of his five-year sentence."

The U.S. government does give attention to the problem of Americans locked up overseas. There are complaints about the effectiveness of that attention because some American prisoners expect more help than they get, more help than the government ever suggests it will or can give. U.S. policy is that Americans involved with the criminal justice system of another country ought to receive at least the same type of treatment normally accorded the nationals of that country. Unfortunately, too often that norm is abysmally low.

Many of the problems American prisoners face in their dealings with embassy and consulate staff are based on understandable human differences. Some consular officers are more interested and motivated, personally and professionally, in prisoners' affairs than others; some consular officers are simply better at their jobs than others. Some consulates and embassies are understaffed, while others have sufficient staff to attempt to meet some of the needs and desires of prisoners. Some prisoners are guilty of crimes that offend the sensibilities of consular officers and affect their attitudes toward offering help. At the same time, other Americans locked up are so obviously victims of unjust circumstances that they elicit extra interest from consulate staffers.

The State Department claims money plays a leading role in the quality of attention Americans can expect to receive from their government overseas. In Chile during 1991, consular officers decided not to visit an American who was locked up two thousand miles from their office. The decision, according to the State Department's inspector general, was based on financial concerns; there wasn't enough money in the budget to warrant such a costly journey. Perhaps the incident was publicized as a ploy by the Bureau of Consular Affairs to rationalize requesting a larger slice of the federal pie. "A consular officer at post," admits Consular Affairs in its annual report to Congress, "indicated to an inspector that the incarcerated American might have been released sooner had a consular officer been available on site to press for expedited processing of the case with local authorities." The report leaves open the possibility that a strained federal budget might "prevent a post from carrying out its responsibilities to American citizens arrested abroad."

But continuing complaints of inadequate assistance also result from a hypocrisy that permeates the foreign policy of the United States. While consular officials around the world shrug their shoulders and tell Americans in prison that there is simply nothing much that the U.S. government can do to help, it is important to remember that when it suits the foreign policy goals of the government, the U.S. stops at nothing to help its citizens—even if they are not in jeopardy and don't ask for help.

Consider, for example, the invasion of Grenada. One of the rationalizations used for the invasion was the plight of a handful of American medical students studying on the island. These students were not prisoners, but the Reagan administration argued forcefully that ensuring the freedom and safety of these students was one of the important factors considered when the decision was made in Washington to send in U.S. troops. After the war, some of the students said they never felt in danger until the marines arrived to rescue them.

Consider also the case of Jennifer Casolo. In November 1989, she was arrested at her home in San Salvador, El Salvador. Police charged her with hiding explosives and ammunition in her back yard for the Faribundo Martí Liberation Front; specifically, they accused her of possessing weapons of war. If convicted she faced a long sentence. The charges, based on a special anti-terrorism law, carried a penalty of up to twenty years in prison. Casolo was twenty-eight at the time; she had been living in El Salvador for the previous four years, working to organize tours for religious and government leaders from the United

States who wanted to study developments in that country's civil war firsthand. She opposed the U.S. foreign policy that provided military and other support to the Salvadoran government in their fight against the Faribundo Martí guerillas and believed that other Americans would reject their government's position if they too saw conditions in El Salvador for themselves.

Despite the official State Department policy that the U.S. government cannot intervene in the cases of Americans arrested overseas who want help from their own government, the United States interceded in the Casolo case. The U.S. involvement was not to assist this U.S. citizen, but to help the police and their case against her. In fact, there may well have been no case against her had the U.S. government not been involved.

The Salvadoran police were ecstatic over the arrest. In announcing his achievement, Colonel Alejandro Sánchez Paredes, the director of the National Police at the time, said that a consular officer from the U.S. embassy joined his men for the raid and arrest. The *New York Times* reporter who covered the story, Lindsey Gruson, reported that a U.S. government official, whom he did not identify, helped with the planning of the raid on Casolo's house. "It's a good bust," Gruson quoted the U.S. official as saying after Casolo was taken off to prison. Reporter Gruson looked at the weapons and characterized them as appearing "to be old and to have been buried for some time, providing some support to the supposition that she might not have been aware of the cache." The human rights organization Americas Watch was appalled by the U.S. involvement in the arrest, immediately criticizing the government not only for implying Casolo was guilty, but also for not helping her defend herself.

The Bush White House further jeopardized Casolo's case. "She's guilty" was the essence of presidential spokesman Marlin Fitzwater's comments to the Associated Press. "There are indications of her involvement, that's for certain," were his exact words. But he didn't stop there. At a time when not just Casolo's liberty, but her life was in danger, Fitzwater blithely bumbled on, augmenting the growing opinion against Casolo. "It's fairly clear that these weapons were found there," he said. "I mean, we're not talking about a small package of pistols here. We're talking about tons of equipment and mortars and dynamite and rounds of ammunition and explosives. This is hardly a case of someone having a few things flipped in their shopping bag on the way home." That they were found in her yard did not make them hers, nor prove she knew they had been buried there, but such details didn't bother the White House. Fitzwater continued, "I don't know what the specific evidence is, but I certainly have read all of the press accounts of some very definitive involvement in terms of her role and past history." Her history included opposition to Bush's foreign policy, but no criminal activity.

Casolo's friends and supporters called the arrest a frame-up, identifying her as a pacifist. The Salvadoran government suffers a long and bloodied history of opposition to any church-related political activities. Casolo was working for a Texas organization called Christian Education Seminars, arranging the tours for interested Americans. She insisted she knew nothing of the hidden weaponry, had only recently moved into the rented house, and was often out of town traveling. "Somebody hates me or somebody is trying to frame me," Casolo told the National Police on a videotaped statement made while the search of her property was taking place. "I don't know who brought this material to my house."

Such claims did not stop the Bush administration from finding her guilty, immediately. From her home state, Connecticut, came an infuriated response from Senator Christopher Dodd. "I am outraged," he said after Fitzwater's announcement, "by comments attributed to U.S. government officials in the last forty-eight hours that assert or even imply Jennifer Casolo is guilty of anything." Dodd accused the Bush administration of ignoring a basic tenet of American law: the presumption of innocence. He correctly labeled the remarks being made by government officials as "unwarranted, prejudicial, and irresponsible," and worried that they could endanger other Americans overseas. "It signaled open hunting," he said later, "not only on Jennifer but on hundreds of other legitimate Americans working with poor refugees."

In fact, during the time Casolo was locked up, at least one other American spent time pacing back and forth in a Salvadoran prison cell. Late 1989 was a period of accelerated guerilla activity there, and the government responded with a crackdown on churches and church workers that it suspected of collaboration with the rebels. Scott Wright, a lay missionary from Lincoln, Nebraska, was among those arrested. He was held without charges being filed and told he would be freed only if he agreed to leave El Salvador. After a weekend in prison, he flew to Texas.

Casolo, held without the possibility of bail, went off to Ilopango Women's Prison, ironically an institution that used to be one of the stops on her tour route. As she waited for her day in court, her own government's embassy staff again made clear that she should not expect help from them. When asked what the influential U.S. mission in San Salvador intended to do next, officials at the embassy told reporters the U.S. role was to "let Salvadoran justice run its course." (At that point, after some ten years of civil war and countless political murders attributed to death squads, the Salvadoran judicial system had no successful prosecutions of these killings to its credit.)

After two weeks of sleeping first on cardboard at the National Police headquarters, then on straw mats with the other women inmates at Ilopango, Casolo was ordered released for lack of evidence and deported. She said she was often blindfolded during threatening interrogation sessions, though never hurt. At a time when the Salvadoran government was spending 1.4 million dollars worth of U.S. foreign aid money a day, it clearly felt Casolo was more risk than she was worth. Senator Dodd—then chairman of the Senate Foreign Relations Committee—strongly lobbied the Salvadoran president for her release.

Once back home, Casolo called the U.S. government's behavior "shameful and disgraceful." She asked a crowd that came to greet her at the airport in New York, "How can the Bush administration say they're fighting for a just society in El Salvador when they don't treat an American citizen with justice?" During her time in custody, she said, she didn't realize the White House was calling her guilty. "I tried to convey to the Salvadoran police that a person is innocent until proven guilty, but I didn't know that American officials weren't giving me that right."

Jennifer Casolo's case was an unusual and extreme example of the U.S. government's response to the needs of an American in trouble abroad. But it is not unique. During the American-instigated military coup that overthrew the elected Allende government in Chile, journalist Charles Horman was arrested by the new regime, held briefly, and executed. The foot-dragging and deceit exercised by U.S. authorities working in Chile at the time are exposed in the chilling Thomas Hauser book *Missing* and the Costa-Gavras film of the same name.

Certainly the official policy of the State Department is to provide U.S. citizens abroad with the most beneficial and efficient services available, and that includes imprisoned Americans. The *Foreign Affairs Manual* specifically states, "Traditionally, one of the basic functions of the consular officer has been to provide a 'cultural bridge' between the host community and the officer's own compatriots traveling or residing abroad.

No one needs that cultural bridge," the State Department reminds its employees, "more than the individual U.S. citizen who has been arrested in a foreign country or imprisoned in a foreign jail."

The manual is firm. "Neither arrest nor conviction deprives a U.S. citizen of the right to the consular officer's best efforts in protecting the citizen's legal and human rights. Consular officers are obliged to assist arrested or imprisoned U.S. citizens with dedicated professionalism, regardless of their own views as to the innocence or guilt of the individuals."

The manual teaches the consular officers about the importance of visiting a prisoner as soon after his or her arrest as possible, not just to assess the status of the prisoner, but because, "Experience has demonstrated that prompt personal access to the detained citizen assures both the arrestee and the host authorities of the serious interest of the U.S. Government in the case." Regular visits—although the exact regularity is no longer specified, it had been at least monthly—are mandatory during the prisoner's pretrial confinement. Officers are forbidden from making "any display of disdain, self-righteousness, or moral disapproval which might impair the relationship with the arrestee." They are cautioned against transmitting in their reports back to Washington "any uncalled-for or gratuitous remarks or comments that might prove embarrassing if required to be released under the Privacy or Freedom of Information Acts."*

U.S. missions abroad are directed by the manual to provide prisoners with a list of local lawyers and information about how the local judiciary system operates. Consular officers are instructed to look for evidence of torture when they meet with the prisoner and determine if the prison meets "generally accepted international standards." If it doesn't, the officer is taught to try intervene with the local authorities to improve the living conditions of the American prisoner.

When Americans started to fill foreign jails in record numbers starting in the early seventies, the State Department made a concerted effort to

---

*The *Foreign Affairs Manual* is the official rulebook for the U.S. Foreign Service. The quotes are from chapter 400 of revised Volume 7, titled "Consular Affairs" and dated October 30, 1984, which was the instructional document in use in January 1992 to guide consular officers through the thicket of problems they face dealing with the arrest of U.S. citizens abroad.

get information out to travelers about the dangers of arrest and imprisonment overseas, especially on drug charges. One such leaflet – designed to appeal to young readers – was called, "It Was Such a Little Amount" (Department of State Publication 8862, General Foreign Policy Series 300, June 1976).

The cover is filled with terrifying anonymous quotes like, "The cell door clanged shut and I found myself in a hole. There were two wooden bunks to sleep in and the roof was open – but barred. There was no stove. It was so cold we could see our breath." Inside the pamphlet, in bold black and white, is the basic information: "Did you know that most countries have much stiffer drug laws than the United States . . . that when you're busted abroad you aren't covered by U.S. laws and constitutional rights . . . that foreign drug laws frequently make no distinction between soft and hard drugs . . . that bail is not granted in most countries in drug-trafficking cases . . . that few provide a jury trial . . . that you need not even be present at your trial." The leaflet warns of long pretrial detention, long sentences after convictions, death penalties. It ends with the stark announcement: "Face the facts, Uncle Sam can't get you out."

By March 1990, the leaflet was renamed "Travel Warning on Drugs Abroad," and included even stronger language. "Once you're arrested," it insists, "the American consular officer CANNOT get you out!" In case the message is missed, it is emphasized again, "The U.S. Consular Officer CANNOT demand your immediate release or *get you out of jail!*"

Thirty Years in Bangkok: "I Am a Beaten Man"

> If you are arrested in Thailand, the American
> consul cannot get you out!
>
> From a sign posted in the U.S. embassy
> in Bangkok, which also reminds
> American travelers that the Thai penalties
> for heroin possession and smuggling
> include capital punishment

|||||||||||||||||||| **N**ot a one is innocent." The U.S. consul I speak with in Bangkok makes no secret of his disgust with the forty or so Americans who are serving time in Thailand for violating drug laws. Sitting behind his sprawling desk in a spacious embassy office, Fred Vogel has a hard time stifling his abhorrence for the prisoners and what they represent to him. He calls them great con artists, great storytellers. "These are not naive kids, even if they're not professional traffickers," Vogel spits out his distaste. "They're perfectly well aware of what they're doing and willing to take the risk."

There are five prisons near Bangkok where Americans live. The maximum security prison is Bangkwang. Shorter-term inmates serve time at Klong Prem, the women at the Women's Remand Home. The Medical Correctional Facility holds narcotics law violators while their cases are investigated, and the Bangkok Special Prison holds criminals convicted of violent crimes.

I hail a cab with an English-speaking driver and head out toward the airport and Bangkwang. The driver translates for me, explaining my interest in meeting with American prisoners, and the first guard lets me into the courtyard of the prison.

Gaining access to Americans in foreign jails is usually a complicated procedure, even if the local authorities allow journalists into their facilities. Unless the inmate signs a complete privacy waiver, the U.S. Privacy Act prevents American embassy officials from providing the names of those held. Most Americans do not sign blanket Privacy Act waivers. Instead, in the hope that their conflicts with foreign laws won't follow them home, they allow only their lawyers and their immediate families access to their files. In such cases, American officials would simply tell me how many Americans were at what prisons and describe the charges against them. Consequently, I often went into prisons without the names of the Americans I wanted to see. This made it difficult to convince the guards that my business was genuine.

At Bangkwang, visitors are meeting with prisoners in long, low open-air buildings, the visitors and the prisoners separated not only by bars, but also by wire mesh screens designed to keep contraband from being exchanged. Before I can attempt to locate any of the Americans, I am evicted by the duty officer as soon as he learns my profession.

As we make our way back to the street, I receive a quick lesson in Thai prison regulations from my driver. His firm advice is to put away my business cards; I'll never get up to the cages identified as a journalist. We get back into the taxi and drive the few kilometers down the road to Klong Prem. I wander into a courtyard scene similar to the one I have just encountered at Bangkwang. But this time, after walking in as if I were a regular, I stay away from the guards while I size up the scene. No one seems to pay any attention to me.

What is most remarkable is the noise. It is impossible to overemphasize the cacophony of screeching Thai voices that fills the courtyard during visiting hours, as families yell back and forth to their locked-up relatives through the wire mesh.

Eventually the routine becomes clear: One guard is at work behind a desk set up in the courtyard. Visitors approach him, they talk, and he writes something on a slip of paper. Then a runner goes inside the prison with the paper and after a wait the prisoner appears.

I approach the guard in charge and try to take advantage of his limited grasp of English. "I am an American," I say. "I want to see American prisoners." With sign language, waving his pad of official forms, he makes it clear that I need the name of a prisoner before I can talk with anyone.

"Just a minute," is my stalling reply and again I stand in the courtyard listening to the screaming, watching, plotting. No one bothers me.

Among the Thai families, a tall, blond, Norwegian woman stands out in the crowd. She is there to visit a foreigner, not an American. But she knows Americans and suggests a name for me to write on the form. I go back to the controlling guard, fill out the paper, and after more waiting am rewarded with a soft-spoken man in his thirties, in his tenth year of a thirty-year sentence for heroin smuggling.

Over and over again, in my journey from country to country, from prison to prison, I have faced an awkward, crucial few moments when a prisoner who was not expecting a visitor was summoned to meet me. They rarely knew why I was there wanting to talk with them. A runner would fetch them, only saying that they had a visitor. Then they would face me, not knowing who I was, and I would have just a few seconds to explain my business and convince them to sit still for an interview.

That's what I am doing with the heroin smuggler in Klong Prem. He tells me he doesn't want to talk, doesn't want to answer my questions. But, as is so often the case when people are asked to speak about themselves, he stays for a while. The tedium of his thirty-year sentence has been broken momentarily by my unexpected arrival. Finally, promising anonymity, promising to use no specifics from his comments that might somehow come back to haunt him, I convince him that it might be of some service to other Americans for him to talk. "You know," he begins, "there's a saying, 'if you can't say anything good, don't say anything.' I do not want to talk at all about conditions here because one way or another it will get back and they will retaliate. Even if it is just by keeping us from having a magazine. One magazine means a lot."

Then he eloquently explains how he's come to appreciate freedom. "People say freedom is just a state of mind. That's not true." He speaks softly, while the Thais around him yell. "Look at us," he says caustically, "we're separated by these bars, and when you've had enough, you can turn around and walk. You've got the freedom to go through that wall, to open your door and look at the stars, to love a woman."

He was correct, I have that freedom and he doesn't. But then, he smuggled heroin and I didn't.

He complains about the U.S. embassy, saying they are of no help to him. He ridicules the efforts of the Drug Enforcement Administration to combat heroin trafficking, suggesting that if it really were the goal of U.S. foreign policy to eradicate the problem, then the poppy-rich

Golden Triangle should be napalmed and its residents resettled and supported.

"I'm a defeated, bitter person," he tells me quietly. Then he offers a few words of advice for travelers, "You're only an American in America," and heads back inside after promising to tell other Americans I am out in the courtyard, available if they want to talk. None come.

"The conditions are shocking when you first come here, really shocking." I am just a few paces down the road from Klong Prem, at the Women's Remand Home listening to the laments of Sherry Work and Cynthia Bridges. These two young American women were convicted of smuggling heroin, too. Sherry is facing a forty-seven-year and six-month sentence, her friend Cynthia a mere twenty years.

Now that I am familiar with the system, I make my way past the first guard at the main gate and am lucky enough to find an Australian woman waiting for a visit. She provides me with American names, I fill out the forms, and within a few minutes the two bubbly women come bounding into the visiting cage announcing, "Peter! Peter! It's so good to see you again!" They tell me they'll be only too happy to talk. Their familiar, enthusiastic greeting is designed to keep the guards from getting suspicious, they say. They had no idea who I was when they were summoned for a visit, but they don't want the guards to think that we don't know each other while they determine why I am at the prison.

At the Women's Remand Home there are two sets of wire-mesh-covered bars with an empty space between them, making it absolutely impossible to pass anything between visitors and prisoners. The distance, combined with the poor acoustics and the high-pitched frenzy of the Thais visiting, creates an odd mood.

I am prepared for that. I have been traveling around the world, making my way into bizarre prisons, and interviewing desperate criminals and unfortunate losers. But I have failed to completely insulate myself from the empathetic emotions I suddenly feel even for these two drug peddlers. I look into the cage at two women my age, from my culture, speaking my slang, and facing a ruined life.

Heroin trafficking is a vile crime, predatory, and selfish. But is over forty-seven years in a Thai prison the appropriate punishment? It is difficult for me, especially when our interview is completed, not to feel some compassion. Their spirit and spunk add to the strange atmosphere.

Sherry tells me about working in the prison kitchen, how she finds it diverting. Cynthia describes her injuries after a fall, and waiting six months for medical attention at a hospital to treat the resulting back problem. They speak approvingly about their guards.

"We get along perfectly well with them," says Cynthia. "They're very playful. As long as you keep them in a good mood, they're okay. You don't give them any problems, they don't bother you."

Sherry points to a guard watching us talk. I am pressed up against the cage, jamming the tiny Walkman-sized tape recorder I have hidden in the pocket of my jacket toward the prisoner's cage. Once I saw that visitors to Thai prisons are not searched, I decided to take along the machine to record the conversations. "This one," says Sherry, "the one with the little foo-foo hairdo right here, one day I was going to court—you have to pass through all these gates—and I got to thinking, 'Shit, I've got on three pairs of earrings, gold, you're not allowed jewelry in here. When I come back in here they're going to take them away.' I just pulled them out of my ears and said, 'Here take these.' She just took them and said, 'Oh!' And then two days later she came inside and gave them back. Most of them are young, they're really cool."

But cool, insists Sherry, doesn't mean corrupt. "I would say there are no guards on the take in this prison. Okay, I know one that will sell nightgowns every two months." It sounds so tame compared with El Sexto and La Mesa. "She'll bring in three or four nightgowns and you can buy them."

The conditions, they agree with consul Vogel, are acceptable. "You can accept them," says Cynthia, "it's a matter of adjustment. I think we're better off than the guys are."

Now converted to Buddhism, Sherry says her religion helps her deal with the long sentence, a sentence she is confident she won't be forced to serve. She's probably right. Most prisoners faced with a life sentence in Thailand get out in about a dozen years, and when I spoke with her, Sherry had already served almost four years. "It doesn't really bother me because I can't imagine being here much longer. I just can't imagine it. I fill my days as well as I can. I work as hard as I can. I learn as much as I can. I really have a good relationship with my own karma, I feel. And I can accept this because I figure, you know, hey, I'll be out of here before long. What time I have here I have to use as a lesson, because I have to be here for a reason. And until I learn that lesson I'm going to damn well sit here." She laughs and adds, "I hope it's soon."

But Sherry feels wronged. She doesn't think she deserves forty-seven years for her crime and blames the Drug Enforcement Administration for convincing the Thai government to deal severely with American drug law violators. She runs through familiar stories of CIA and DEA involvement in drug trafficking when it suited the needs of U.S. policy-makers. "Now, they changed the laws to these incredible sentences. Maybe one half the people in this jail are here for heroin and life sentences, there are over a hundred. And murder cases – whap, bam, three years, five years, nothing. I mean murder's nothing."

Sherry, as Vogel suggested, is the first to admit she's no naive kid, no Chris Rincon. She estimates she made about twenty drug runs – mostly marijuana and hashish – over some fifteen years before she was caught. She blames her arrest, with contempt in her voice, not remorse, on a "snitch." But she insists the drugs she and her fellow inmates transported over the years are just a drop in the bucket compared with the quantities the really big operators move. And these big-time professionals, she's sure, don't get caught because they're so well connected.

"Right now every person in this prison, any prison, is eligible to apply for a royal pardon." Sherry's voice rises as she gets upset. "The Americans will never receive one because of the DEA, because they've said, 'Now listen, King baby, no.' So the Americans don't get royal pardons. Now all these other people sitting here, I'm speaking French, Italian, Spanish, German, like this, three years, four years maximum and they're out the door. The Americans sit, sit, sit, nine years like this. It's just incredible. The American embassy will not support us for this alternative way out of here."

The American government is not going out of its way to help criminals like Sherry. In fact, U.S. authorities often work with the Thai police, investigating and arresting Americans involved in heroin trafficking. "Let them sit," is how she sums up what feels like abandonment to her.

Consul Vogel is irritated with the U.S. government, too, but for the opposite reason. "We as a government," he says about his own country, "are not consistent. While we're lenient in the U.S. with our own citizens, we expect other countries to be tough." He heartily approves of the severe Thai response.

It's an attitude Sherry rejects as wrong, "We're human beings and we're American citizens. That makes a lot of difference; I don't think anyone should ever be looked on as a dog. And I think some of the people at the embassy definitely look on us like we're dogs." Cynthia chimes in, "They say we're 'scum of the earth.' "

Consul Vogel rejects the charges, "We would never consider an American citizen scum of the earth or any different from another American citizen." But he expresses no sympathy for locked-up smugglers like Sherry. "The mules," he says of Sherry and her ilk, "are not the kingpins. But the heroin couldn't be smuggled without them. So it's at least putting a dent in the problem." There should be severe penalties, he believes, because severe penalties cut smuggling activity and consequently reduce the availability of heroin on the streets of America.

From behind her bars, Sherry Work disagrees. "Okay, we broke the law. I think being in this place for four years is just about enough, thank you." The resentment rings through the cage as the guard signals the end of visiting time.

"Be cool," calls Sherry as she and Cynthia head back inside.

Americans are imprisoned elsewhere in East Asia, although not in such high numbers as in Thailand.

In rigid Japan, visiting prisoners is impossible for me. The foreign ministry claims any attention given to American inmates in Japanese jails might rekindle memories of Japanese treatment of American World War II prisoners of war.

Maximum security Fuchu Prison is where Americans held in Japan are confined, in a wing separated from the Japanese prisoners except during working hours. Unlike their compatriots in so many other foreign jails, the Americans make no complaints to U.S. officials about sanitary conditions. They say they are not physically beaten. The frustrations inside Fuchu take on a distinctly Japanese flavor.

They live in individual cells, with metal beds and a mattress, a desk and a reading lamp, and a toilet. There is a library with English-language books available. Smoking is not allowed, nor are television sets permitted in the cells. Communal television viewing time is rigidly restricted, as is exercise time.

Western-style food is available. The Americans are offered coffee and bread for breakfast, for example, instead of the tea and rice the Japanese inmates receive. Dinner might be pork soup and vegetables, fried fish, potato salad, bread, tomatoes, and yogurt. Lunch and dinner include more meat than the Japanese convicts' diet, and some of the Americans, according to U.S. officials, come out of Fuchu heavier than they arrived.

Not all of them. Ed Arnett was sent to Fuchu after being convicted of possessing two kilograms of marijuana. When he got out he told *Parade* magazine, "I didn't know I could still cry until I went to prison in Japan." He complained about his censored mail, not being allowed to write, being restricted to reading books approved by prison authorities, and a diet he remembers as being mostly seaweed, fish, and rice.

But, like so many Americans in prison overseas, Arnett broke the law, and he figured he was treated harshly, but fairly. "The guards at Fuchu were hard, but they never messed with you unless there was a reason," he said. "You didn't have to worry about the other prisoners coming after you, either. And the laws of Japan are for everybody. That's the main thing."*

In Japan, as is the case in so much of the world, criminal suspects can expect to be held without bail during pretrial detention. They do not enjoy the services of a lawyer during interrogation, and their trial is before a judge only. There is no jury.

"The situation is severe," U.S. consul Ed McKeon tells me in Tokyo. He visits the Americans in Fuchu regularly as part of his official duties. "I don't think Americans are used to living in such a highly disciplined environment." Silence is enforced during meals and work periods. There is no heat in the prison, and the suburbs of Tokyo, where Fuchu is located, get cold in the winter. The Americans pile on several layers of long underwear and keep their gloves on inside. Frostbite is a problem.

"It's not unkind," says McKeon as he tries to describe the conditions he sees. "You'll never be maltreated. No one has ever said they were beaten or abused or harassed. It's just that it's a strict, disciplined society." Then McKeon makes a comment that I have heard more than once from American prisoners abroad and their visitors. "If I had to be in jail," he says, "I'd rather be in jail here than back in America," pointing to the violence in U.S. prisons as worse than the austerity of Fuchu.

At least one American went to jail in Japan as a matter of conscience. A law in Japan that all foreigners over sixteen years of age must be fingerprinted if they stay in the country over a year offended U.S. citizen Kathleen Morikawa. Since among Japanese citizens, only criminals were required to be fingerprinted, Morikawa considered the law offen-

---

*Ed Arnett was interviewed for the January 15, 1984, issue of *Parade* by author and lawyer James Webb once he returned home to Omaha, Nebraska, from Fuchu.

sive and discriminatory. Morikawa was offered the choice between a fine of about forty dollars or five days in jail for breaking the law. She chose jail, saying, "It's not a matter that can be solved by paying ten thousand yen so I'd rather follow my conscience and pay it by serving five days in prison."

Aside from any prisoners of war who may still be held in Vietnam, at least a few Americans have been detained by Vietnamese authorities since the war there ended. Two were arrested for entering the country illegally.

Bill Mathers, a partner in a marine construction company, denies he ever even entered Vietnamese waters while sailing his yacht from Singapore to Hong Kong. He was about thirty-six miles off the Vietnamese coast when he was stopped, forced to a Vietnamese port, and held for both violating territorial waters and espionage charges.

Mathers's boat was hailed by a fishing vessel filled with armed Vietnamese troops. They ordered him to pull their boat to shore with his eighty-foot yacht. He made the lines between the two vessels fast, then went below to his cabin and got on the radio announcing a frantic mayday. But one of the soldiers heard him, broke his radio, and forced him at gunpoint over to the fishing boat.

"They tied my arms behind my back," Mathers remembers months later when he is free again, "tied me up to a post, and got out an M-16 machine gun." His laugh as he tells this part of the story of his capture is sardonic. "They fired a couple of rounds from that and pointed it at my chest. I remained that way for the next two or three hours. Then they untied my arms from behind me and tied me up with my hands in front of me for another hour and then they let me sit on the back of the boat in an untied condition." Mathers and his crew could find no common language in which to speak to the boarding party. All the communication was done with sign language.

He denies spying for either side. "They told me I had two options," he says of the interrogation he faced once he was on shore. "They said I could go to prison for an unspecified period and I could have my boat confiscated and all the equipment on it confiscated. I could also go to a public trial that would be designed to embarrass my parents, my company, and my friends. They told me that recently there had been some public trials of a group of Vietnamese that had been plotting to overthrow the government. They said three of those individuals had been sentenced to execution. The implication was there that that was a possibility if I went to a trial." The grim trial scenario was the first option Mathers was offered by his captors.

"The alternative to that," he explains, "was to agree to undertake activities in a strictly confidential manner. They would not inform my government, they would not inform my family." He says the Vietnamese wanted him to get them information on U.S. military maneuvers in East Asia. They wanted him to learn about any plotting against the Vietnamese government that was going on in Vietnamese refugee camps in Southeast Asia. And they wanted the results of any offshore oil exploration that American oil companies conducted during the Vietnam War.

"Most people," says Mathers, "would say, 'Okay, I agree,' and then wait until you get out." But Mathers says that aside from his philosophical rejection of the idea of spying for the Vietnamese, he didn't want to take the risk of going along with their offer simply as a device to get out of their custody. In addition to his decision not to take a chance that the Vietnamese would somehow compromise him if he agreed to be their spy even if only as a ruse to escape, Mathers was concerned about his boat. The Vietnamese were dealing with a typically idiosyncratic American. "They were going to keep the vessel in safe keeping," he says of his yacht. "And if I performed adequately, I would eventually get it back."

Well, Mathers had invested his life savings in the classic schooner. He was not about to jeopardize the *So Fong*. "I refused to spy for them. I said, 'No, period.' And they said, 'You're on your way to prison. This investigation is finished and you're going to prison.' They came back the next day and said, 'Now you've had a night to think about it, what do you say?' And I said, 'No!' "

Mathers credits pressure from the State Department – and family, friends, and colleagues all over the world – for the decision by the Vietnamese finally to release him after his parents accepted the demand that they pay ten thousand dollars. The situation was not resolved quickly. Mathers spent almost nine months in solitary confinement in a military barracks, allowed out of his room only to use the toilet. And the *So Fong* stayed in Vietnam when he finally flew home.

Mathers's routine in prison started daily with a cup of coffee and a piece of bread at seven in the morning. A bowl of vegetable soup came at eleven, along with some meat, a pineapple, a cucumber, and one tomato. It was the same every day. "When you have that much time to think about things," he says he learned during his captivity, "you begin to realize that owning a boat like that is not so important. The material possessions aren't so important. It's friends and family and your work that are the important things. I've been very lucky. There's no feeling of anger at all. It's just a great feeling of disappointment."

He tells a story to illustrate his point. "There was an old lady who befriended me – she was the cook, she couldn't speak any English, but she was extremely well respected by the other people because she was apparently some hero of the Viet Cong. She had also spent thirteen years in prison. She was the only one who made a gesture toward me. She was very friendly to me. There are many people like that in Vietnam, as there are in every country." Then he talks about all the time he spent alone, denied even visitors and mail, prevented from gaining any contact with the rest of the world. "I just think it's extraordinarily sad that people have to live under a government that acts the way they do. It was the sign almost of an uncivilized nation what they did. This concept of having access to prisoners is something which is accepted by all civilized countries."

After his release he speaks calmly about the episode. "I was treated all right. I had plenty of food and – a phrase they liked – I always had freedom of my own space."

A teenage American treasure hunter knows about those Vietnamese spaces, too. Californian Frederick Graham was enticed to join a search party for some of Captain Kidd's buried booty. But the map they used led Graham and his party to a tiny island off Phu Quoc, an island in the Gulf of Siam that is part of Vietnam. Whether or not Captain Kidd ever sailed in the Gulf of Siam, let alone buried any treasure there, is a matter of continuing speculation among historians and treasure hunters less impetuous than young Graham.

Before the search party began any serious digging, they were seized and charged with illegally landing on Vietnamese territory. In addition to losing their vessel and all their equipment, they, too, were each charged a ten-thousand-dollar fine. It took almost a year for Graham's family to raise the money and arrange his release, time that Graham, too, spent in solitary confinement.

Another American claims he was just taking a swim as a tourist in Thailand when he came to shore in Laos by mistake. Jon Robert Phillips was sunbathing when Laotian soldiers took him into custody. He was held for a few days and released without complaining. "My guards were warm, friendly," he says. "They were sympathetic to my situation; they met all my basic needs and tried to cheer me up."

Naturalized American citizens returning to their native countries for a visit often are susceptible to the whims of irritated governments. Some governments punish the change in allegiance. A San Francisco doctor who was born in Vietnam, Bui Duy Tam, learned that lesson when he got off the plane in his native country for a scheduled three-week stay with his mother. Instead of the family visit, he ended up spending more than two months in jail in Hanoi, charged with "bringing materials detrimental to national security" into Vietnam. Accused of being a political subversive, Dr. Bui spent his confinement facing endless interrogation. "We worked very hard," said the fifty-six-year-old from his wheelchair at the airport, "in the morning, afternoon, and sometimes in the evening. I think that is why I became ill."

His release came as the result of political pressure placed on the Vietnamese government when it was attempting to improve relations with Washington as part of its strategy for dealing with the disintegration of the Communist world. "I'm so very grateful to be home," the doctor told reporters who greeted him at the San Francisco airport. "I am very proud to be Vietnamese," he explained, "but I am also very proud to be a naturalized citizen of the United States, where freedom and human rights are considered of utmost importance."

As U.S. military bases close in the Philippines and American servicemen are transferred home, fewer Americans will be dealing with the Philippine police. Not that such encounters have been much of a problem over the years of close U.S. involvement in the political affairs of the former colony.

"Most of the cases are worked out informally," is the understatement from one U.S. military official, explaining the cash system of justice often at work in the streets of the Philippines. It has been one of the few countries in the world where an American in trouble with the law can escape by flashing a wad of dollars and announcing, "Hey, I'm an American."

American servicemen and tourists do get in trouble with the law frequently. Manila and other Philippine cities, especially those near the bases, are wide-open sin cities, catering to all tastes in sex and intoxication. Yet it has been rare for an American lawbreaker to go to jail.

|||||||||||||||||||||||||||| Bui Duy Tam surrounded by his family on his return to San Francisco from Vietnam. A naturalized U.S. citizen, he was detained when he traveled to Vietnam to visit his mother. (Photo: Kim Komenich)

Usually those from the military are sent back to the bases, perhaps after paying cash for whatever damages they caused. Civilians, too, can usually buy their way out of all but the most serious situations.

Consider the case of airman Bankie Howard, charged when Marcos ran the Philippines with raping seven underage girls in Olongapo. Olongapo is the party strip on Subic Bay, filled with licensed "hospitality girls" selling themselves to the Americans. Facing a possible 147 years behind bars, he was finally sentenced to one year at hard labor.

I sit in the Spider's Web in Manila's "hospitality girl" district, looking for Lieutenant Eddie's girlfriend. She works at the bar; he's a guard at Manila City Jail who is a friend of an American reporter living and working in Manila. Lieutenant Eddie is supposed to provide me with a tour of City Jail and locate any Americans who might be locked up there.

While I wait, I hear stories about wild drinking, about the drugs and sex available to all the cruising Americans in Manila, servicemen and tourists. And I hear again that if an American causes trouble, he's expected to pay off whomever he offends, not go to jail. Eddie doesn't appear, so I head down to the jail on my own.

Getting through the barred jail door is no problem, despite my cameras and tape recorders. Visitors are marked with an identifying rubber stamp to differentiate them from the inmates. This day there are no Americans being held. The last one was in and out a few weeks before for a common Manila charge: exploitation of minors.

This trip, I am traveling with a network expense account, so I eat a magnificent breakfast at the luxurious Manila Hotel – grilled garlic-covered fish, mounds of rice, plates full of exotic fruits, mango juice – and go to the taxi stand. The temperature is perfect, the sunshine glinting off the pristine pool. But even the colonial Manila Hotel can't insulate guests from the stark contrasts of the Philippines, from the political and economic inequities. Guests are checked for weapons by guards at the door. Across the street from these fancy accommodations, homeless Philippine families squat on the edge of the golf course, sleeping out, cooking meals on open grills, their filthy children begging for a few coins.

My taxi driver is an off-duty policeman. Again I am told – this time with disgust – how Americans just buy freedom. He explains how his superior officers order him and his fellow officers to follow this double standard of locking up Filipinos but not Americans. He says that most offenses by Americans are by drunks at bars, and that when there is trouble, the police instruct the Americans to buy out the injured parties.

We head out of jammed Manila toward maximum security New Bilibib Prison. Sex and violence are on display throughout the city. The movie marquees feature oversized, surreal Technicolor paintings of fight scenes from the films being shown. Passengers push for space on a bus. We leave downtown on a toll highway through the suburbs, passing billboards such as the lingerie ad with the legend, "All you have to be is a woman."

The drive takes about an hour, as we move into the tropical countryside. We head into the hills, finally bouncing up a dirt track, past a No Hunting sign, and on into the National Penitentiary compound. As we drive onto the grounds, the guards show only a cursory interest in us; they do not search the taxi.

Adjacent to New Bilibib is medium security Camp Sampagita. Squawking chickens wander around the open-air offices. Here there is not even a rubber stamp. A guard marks my arm with a ballpoint pen, my identification as a visitor. A few trusties—prisoners trusted by the warden— scurry about the camp, looking for Americans. All they finally find is a guy whose parents are U.S. nationals. He wants to talk, but so do most inmates behind bars.

New Bilibib is a white stucco prison, built in 1937. Again, my bag is not searched; no one is concerned about my recording equipment. The guard at the open main gate simply makes the routine request that I check any "sidearms" I might be carrying. I wait in the warden's office while a runner goes off to fetch the lone American inmate on the roster. It feels like 1937 – the dimly lit room, the utilitarian wooden office furniture, the fading black-and-white photographs on the walls commemorating moments in the prison's history.

An old man shuffles in, Placito Santo Tomás. His accent is thick; he's a naturalized ethnic Philippine. Back in the fifties he worked at the White House "for Eisenhower," he proudly tells me. When he came back to the Philippines, he killed his wife and he's been serving his life sentence since 1968. He's happy with U.S. consular officers. Periodically they show up at New Bilibib, provide him with some medicine, and ask him how he's doing. He is doing okay.

Certainly not all the Americans who encounter Philippine justice manage an easy exit. One of the exceptions to the often successful "Hey, I'm an American" defense was Dominique Adams, a twenty-two-year-old tourist when she was arrested in late 1989. It was her first trip out of the United States. To offset the costs, she took a courier job. She agreed to escort a load of automobile parts. Unfortunately, she was not dealing with a reputable operation and she was – unknown to her – loaded with contraband.

At the Manila airport, security guards routinely X-rayed the shipment. Inside the auto parts they found guns secreted, welded to the parts. Adams was taken to jail, charged, and released on bail with the stipulation that she remain in Manila.

Although her lawyer, Richard Atkins of the law firm International Legal Defense Counsel, was confident he had built a sound case proving her innocence, Adams had contacted a reporter for the television show "Inside Edition." Convinced by the reporter that she was in jeopardy of losing at the trial, Adams disappeared into the Philippine jungle just before her court date. She and the reporter – who was fired by "Inside Edition" before the story was broadcast – hired a boat and she successfully escaped from the archipelago.

The court was disgusted with her flight. She was found guilty of the smuggling charges. "Flight is evidence of guilt," explained the judge. Dominique Adams is safely back in America, and there is no extradition treaty between the two countries. But she is a fugitive from justice in the Philippines and cannot return there without facing prison.

There are probably few Americans in prison overseas more foolish or luckier than Kerry Lane Wiley. At the age of thirty-seven, too old to use impetuous youth as an excuse, Wiley decided to move to Malaysia, try to find work teaching computer science, and do a little exploring in the jungles.

Nowhere in the world are the drug laws more severe than in Malaysia and the neighboring city-state, Singapore. Since 1983, hanging by the neck until dead has been the mandatory penalty for drug trafficking in Malaysia, and carrying more than seven ounces of marijuana is considered drug trafficking. Holding that same quantity in Wiley's California hometown would probably result in merely a citation. Even before the law changed, making capital punishment mandatory for traffickers, Malaysia was hanging smugglers, a policy that became an option for the courts in 1975. The law was changed to mandatory hanging in 1983 because the government was distressed that so many judges were sentenc-

|||||||||||||||||||||||||| Tourist Dominique Adams waits as the Philippine police tabulate the guns hidden in her baggage. (Photo: AP/Wide World Photos)

ing smugglers to life in prison instead of to the death penalty. Once the new regulations went into effect, the Deputy Home Affairs Minister Radzi Sheikh Ahmad enthusiastically announced, "I want to hang one a week, hopefully."

Kerry Wiley wasn't listening. When he was arrested in Kuala Lumpur in late 1989, it looked as if Wiley was going to make dubious history as the first American to be executed under Malaysia's law requiring the death penalty for *dadah* traffickers. *Dadah* is a government-usurped word in Malaysia. The word traditionally meant any drug, but as the government campaign against illegal narcotics stepped up in the early eighties, *dadah* was chosen as the term to identify prohibited drugs. In Bahasa Malaysian, the official Malaysian language, the word carries the connotation of repulsiveness.

Malaysia does not hide its harsh penalties for drug trafficking. All visitors to the country, before they cross customs, must fill out an immigration card adorned with the announcement: "Death! That's the mandatory sentence for any *dadah* trafficker in Malaysia. So be forewarned." The same dire warning is emblazoned across the facade of Pudu Prison in Kuala Lumpur, where Wiley sat for over a year, contemplating his bleak future.

According to court records—Wiley refused all requests to be interviewed—Wiley mailed himself a package from Bangkok to Kuala Lumpur. Inside was about a pound of marijuana. He went to the post office to pick it up, signed for it, and was taken into custody. An alert postal clerk had called the police, suspicious because there was no customs declaration form filled out on the package and because the name on the return address was the same as the name of the person to whom the package was sent.

This was not the first time Kerry Lane Wiley faced legal and police problems because of his affinity for marijuana. At home in Sacramento in 1974, he spent three years on probation and paid a 625-dollar fine after police pulled thirteen marijuana plants out of his garden. When he moved to Hawaii in 1986, police at the Honolulu airport found plastic bags stuffed with more than two pounds of marijuana scattered around his luggage. The penalty that time was probation, because of legal questions about the propriety of the baggage search.

Perhaps his earlier experiences gave Wiley the kind of mindless courage needed to violate drug laws that mandate hanging. But Malaysia feels free about hanging *dadah* law violators, despite their nationality.

Singaporean, Thai, Filipino, Australian, Indonesian, and British convicted *dadah* smugglers have all died on the Malaysian gallows since
1975. If anything, the Malaysians seem to be going out of their way to
add some foreigners to the mix, just to prove that they do not dis-
criminate when it comes to execution. The Malaysian courts have made
it a point to ignore the pleas of foreign governments, including one from
the Queen of England, that their wayward citizens be spared the noose.

Wiley insisted to the courts that he was no trafficker, that the marijuana was for his own use. His mother flew out to Kuala Lumpur from
California to testify at his trial, telling the sad story of Wiley's childhood
fall from a cliff in 1964. "The newspapers called it the Christmas mira-
cle," she told the court. "He fell sixty feet down a mountain and was very
lucky to survive. There were angels there." There were also drugs there.
For the next four years Wiley underwent several operations all over his
body. "He was given tranquilizers and painkillers," said Mom, "but after a while he didn't want them."

What he did want was marijuana. He switched from the commercial
drugs to smoking the plant, he testified, to ease the pain from his injuries. He admitted he sent himself the package of marijuana, but only for
his own "medicinal" use. What he failed to explain was how he could
be so mindless as to pick Malaysia—out of all the countries in the
world—to practice his self-medicated lifestyle.

The judge accepted the argument. "The amount of cannabis," said
Judge Shaik Daud, "indicates to me that it was for the personal use of
the accused." Nonetheless the judge sent Wiley to prison for five years,
saying, "Whether it is for personal use or trafficking, drug possession is
still an offense in this country." The sentence was not just five years, it
was five years and ten lashes with a bamboo cane. Those who know say
the cane strokes are excruciatingly painful and Wiley decided to appeal
the sentence and conviction to the Malaysian Supreme Court. Until the
court gets around to reviewing his case, Wiley stays locked up, but is
spared the whipping.

In Singapore, even chewing gum can land the unsuspecting in prison.
In an attempt to keep the city free of sticky used gum, the manufacture,
sale, and importation of gum is now illegal. Violating the gum ban law
can result in a year behind bars. Although the possession of small
amounts of gum for personal chewing is still permitted, tourists must
declare theirs on a customs form.

|||||||||||||||||||||||| **K**erry Lane Wiley on his way to court in Kuala Lumpur. Facing the death penalty for marijuana trafficking, Wiley escaped the noose by claiming the drug was for his own use. (Photo: AP/Wide World Photos)

Inshallah: How the Boyd Brothers Came Home from Peshawar with All Their Hands and Feet

> I hope you've learned that the State Department
> is worthless.
>
> Patricia Saddler to the author, 1991

|||||||||||||||||||| **D**aniel and Charles Boyd have only been home from Pakistan for a week when they sit in their lawyer's luxurious offices along the Potomac River in Washington talking about their misadventure. They laugh, they pray, and they rage for almost three hours, telling their story.

"The judge was laughing at us." Daniel remembers the moment when the sentence was pronounced. "He tells us, 'I have found you guilty.' " Daniel says at that moment he heard a gasp pass through the audience in the courtroom.

"The judge said, 'Your right hand from the wrist, your left foot from the ankle, and you'll spend five years in rigorous imprisonment, and 100,000 rupees fine,' and he looks at me and says, 'for you another five years' for the gun."

"And there was bawling in the courtroom," Charles recalls the tears of the spectators.

Daniel smiles at the memories from the safety of Washington. "It didn't scare us a bit because this was the work of God. If God wanted our hands off, they'd be off. And they're not." He holds his hands over the desk and displays them.

Daniel was smiling the month before, too, as he and Charles walked from the courtroom in Peshawar, sentenced and facing amputation and years of bleak prison time. His explanation for it all is a simple, *"Inshallah."* If God wills it.

Peshawar is a tough border town, combining international intrigue with the atmosphere of the wild old American West and an endless history of tribal infighting and foreign conquest. This capital of the North West Frontier is the last stop for the Pakistani central government. Traditional tribal leaders are still in charge as soon as you leave town.

When the Soviet Union invaded Afghanistan, Peshawar became the staging point for *mujahadin* war-party forays across the Hindu Kush back into Afghanistan, and it became home to whole cities of Afghan refugees who came across the border to escape the fighting. Peshawar also became the headquarters for adventurers, from journalists to relief workers helping the refugees, to U.S. government operatives supplying the *mujahadin* with weapons.

Water buffalo share the rutted streets with honking cars and trucks. Double-decker busses, long retired from service in London, labor through the mass of humanity, animals, and traffic; their paint long gone, hunks of rusty sheet metal patches hanging from their weary sides. Men squat by the side of the road relieving themselves; veiled women dart through the crowds.

At the Deans Hotel, the overhead fans turn slowly; a request from a foreigner procures a couple of cold beers. A few kilometers outside Peshawar, in the foothills heading to the Khyber Pass, opium poppies loll in the breeze, handworkers hammer pot metal into cheap copies of Kalashnikovs and Springfields, and tent cities of Afghan refugees fight the dust and heat.

The Boyd brothers, suburban Virginians, clearly never expected to lose their hands and feet when they went off to practice their religion in an Islamic society. But, like most of the resident Peshawar expatriate community, they weren't naive innocents either. Daniel smiles slyly when he's pushed about exactly what kind of relief work the brothers were doing with the Afghans. This son of a career U.S. Marines officer talks vaguely about choosing Pakistan as his new home because there he could "fight Communism." He alludes to working with Afghans inside Afghanistan during firefights with the Soviets. He suggests he was fighting, too, calling his activities "covert work as a novice."

Certainly American mercenaries, volunteers, and all sorts of agents plied the wild border between Afghanistan and Pakistan during the war, just as they fill Central America and all the other world flashpoints. Daniel even agrees that the bank robbery case against the Boyd brothers may have been a setup by someone or some agency that wanted to remove them from the Afghan war zone.

But whatever the details of their tasks among the Afghans, their brush with the Pakistani legal system was a harrowing interlude they never expected when they set up housekeeping on a Peshawar side street. "We came here because we wanted to be in an Islamic country and wished to raise our children in an Islamic way," Daniel's wife explained during the brothers' trial. She spoke about choosing Peshawar as a better place than Virginia to rear her children, because in America, "they have movies about people eating people. Allah," she said, "gave us the whole world to seek out what we need to seek out."

After the brothers were sentenced to suffer the amputations her reaction was less enthusiastic. "I guess we're just living in a nightmare come true," she allowed.

Charles is the older of the two men, just thirty when he got back from Pakistan, and with his thick beard, introverted eyes, and Pakistani garb—baggy trousers, a tailored shirt with long tails worn out—he looks out of place in the lawyer's offices. Daniel, in his early twenties, is much more animated, filling his story with a combination of American slang and a periodic "*Inshallah.*" His attire is much more of a cultural hybrid. Daniel looks like the young American he is, wearing just a touch of his travels—an Afghan cap—along with a camouflage jacket, jeans, combat boots, and a work shirt.

"We had gone to the mosque to make our prayers," Charles begins. "We prayed. We left the mosque, went into a store and were drinking a Pepsi when we notice the police coming. We were saying to each other, 'It looks like they're going to pick up someone.' We were sitting on the refrigerator for the sodas and they kept coming at us and we said to each other, 'It looks like they're going to pick us up!' "

They were led out into the street and to a waiting police truck, and told that there was some dispute pending regarding their last landlord and that they must come along to the police station. There they were brought before the neighborhood police chief, who was the first to bring up the bank robbery. "We have eight witnesses who say you are the two who did it," he told them.

"We thought maybe he was joking," Charles remembers from the safety and freedom of America. He and Daniel describe the scene in that little Peshawar police station interrogation room where they first realized they were facing serious trouble. They tell of a bland room, the walls covered with old, fading white paint. The chief's desk is decorated with captured trophies: guns, a small bag of heroin. There is one little framed photograph on the desk; it is of Pelé, the Brazilian soccer star. The concrete floor is littered with spittle. There is a Kipling quote up on the wall. Charles recites it as best he can recall, "In the business where there is a superior over an inferior, the inferior never forgets it and the superior never remembers it."

The chief took out his gun and laid it on the desk and told the Boyds again, "We have eight witnesses who say you are the ones that went into that bank."

Daniel makes an effort to paint a picture of just how offensive he found the police chief. "He's a really sinister man," he tells me. "This guy is out of a book for real, his moustache is down to the floor. He didn't speak very good English, but he thought he did." He keeps trying to conjure up a vivid image, "He had beady little eyes. You could see him relishing his power."

Finally Charles comes up with the definitive American example, "You know Yosemite Sam? That attitude describes him exactly."

During that first period of questioning, Yosemite Sam – his Urdu name is Raziq – made the brothers believe that their arrest was a simple shakedown, that if they paid an adequate bribe, they'd be out the door and back at home directly. Raziq, they say, told them that if they gathered "a large sum of money," ostensibly to pay back what was lost in the bank robbery, their problems with him would be over. "He was telling us the fix was in," is Daniel's interpretation.

As they sat there in the police station, Raziq leaned across his desk and bizarrely announced, "Fuck Pakistan. I really want to go to South Africa." It was another indication for the brothers that all they had to do was come up with enough baksheesh and they'd be set free.

News accounts of the Boyds' trial and their life in Peshawar indicate there was a dispute between the United Bank Limited in Hyatabad and the Boyds, and that there was a robbery later at the bank. In June 1991, five thousand dollars arrived from the United States to help the brothers maintain themselves and their families in Pakistan. Both are married;

Daniel and his wife have three little children: Mohammed Nuruddin, Zakaria, and Luqman. The families–all of them had converted to Islam–moved together to Pakistan. They say the idea was to practice their religion in an Islamic country and work to help the Afghan refugees struggling in Pakistan.

They not only adopted the religion, but also took Muslim names. Daniel picked Saifulla Abu Laith, Charles sometimes called himself Asadullah, sometimes Abdul Azziz Sabor. Their wives wrapped themselves in the full black veils customary for Pakistani Muslim women, leaving just their eyes exposed. Debra became Aziza, Sabrina chose Siddiqa. "We became Muslims because it is the purest religion," was Sabrina's explanation. She is Daniel's wife, and it was she who took the five thousand dollars to the bank.

Once there, it seems that one of the bank's managers convinced her to endorse the check over to him, saying that he would cash it on the black market and obtain a better exchange rate for her than the official bank rate. When she came back to the bank for her rupees, the manager claimed she never gave him a check and refused to give her any money.

She went home, fetched the brothers, and they confronted the manager. Accounts differ; some say the bank man paid some of the five thousand to the Boyds. But the family was not satisfied.

It was shortly after that encounter that the United Bank was robbed. Two men showed up at the bank, witnesses for the state testified, armed and appearing to be foreigners dressed as Afghans. There was a shootout with a bank guard and some eighty thousand rupees were stolen. At the official rate that was about thirty-two hundred dollars. Police claimed that during their investigation they recovered about half the missing rupees.*

The Boyds consistently avow that they are innocent of the charges. Certainly they are not the only foreigners in Peshawar who dress like locals. When I was in the North-West Frontier, reporting on the Soviet invasion of Afghanistan, I wandered through the hectic, dusty *suq* and bought an outfit: the distinctive Afghan rolled wool cap, long-tailed shirt, and baggy drawstring trousers. Most Westerners I met along the

---

*Correspondent Steve Coll covered the Boyds' story from Peshawar for the *Washington Post*. There was a strong local angle for the *Post;* the brothers grew up across the Potomac in northern Virginia. Omar Amer reported unsympathetically from the trial for the Pakistani paper *The Nation*. Reports of the September 1991 trial also appeared in the *Muslim* and the *Frontier Post,* two other English-language Pakistani papers.

border packed the same costume in their luggage when they came home. They either used it to disguise themselves as locals for the illegal cross-ing into Afghanistan, or brought it home as a souvenir. Or both.

But the day the Boyd brothers were arrested and offered a chance to buy their way free of what they obviously perceived to be a dangerous setup, Charles and Daniel told Raziq—Yosemite Sam—that they'd pay.

With a police escort, Daniel went home and dug up thirty thousand rupees. "Six months' rent money," he calls it. Back at the police station, he turned the cash over to Raziq, who winked and announced, "Now, you're under Pakistan law." The implication, thought the Boyds at the time, was that they would spend a week or so in jail while their case passed through the corrupt system and was tossed out.

That first day in the jail they asked for the opportunity to wash before their prayers. The sloping floor of their cell was the bathroom, covered with "literally four inches of fecal matter," says Daniel. Their request was denied by Raziq, who told them, "There is nothing wrong with this toilet because this shit is human shit. It is your shit and my shit. It is of you and me. If it was dog shit," Daniel remembers the speech as end-ing, "then you could complain."

As they tell their story, Daniel does most of the talking, with Charles and their mother, Patricia Saddler, interjecting a comment or detail periodically. The words come fast, a mixture of their story, disgust with American politics, praise for Allah, and juvenile American-style humor. They tell of another nickname they concocted for Raziq. They called him Roscoe, after Roscoe P. Coletrane, the sheriff on the television se-ries "The Dukes of Hazzard" who was always chasing the errant Duke brothers.

They laugh in the Washington lawyer's office at the memory, and sing a line from the show's theme song, "We're just the Duke boys, never doin' no harm!" Their mother chimes in, "Too bad you didn't have their car."

After they paid their bribe, they were marched in chains through the rough streets of Peshawar. People called out at them, "Those are the Americans who robbed the bank."

"Inside our heads," says Daniel, "we thought this is just a test from our God."

"But I can see how the typical American would feel," says his brother. Daniel agrees, "But we were ready to die for our belief."

"It was a gift from God," Charles then calls the arrest, "because it made us realize you can't change what God wants. It was a test of faith and patience."

Their references to their faith in God escalate as one outdoes the other trying to explain how their trauma, while they marched in chains toward Peshawar Central Prison, was kept under control by their religion. "Even if I was in a box with my hands and feet gone," says Charles, "I'd say, 'Thank you!' "

"I knew their faith was sustaining them," says Patricia.

For the next several weeks, Central Prison was home. The toilet was infested with worms and roaches. The brothers slept on bricks and made do with food and clothes brought by their families. They weren't manhandled themselves, but tell stories of abuse suffered by fellow prisoners, particularly one teenage Afghan boy. "They had him chained above the window. His arms are up," says Daniel, "so he can't sleep. When his head came down, they slapped him and burned his arms with a cigarette lighter."

The Boyds had been behind bars for three months when their case came to trial before Justice Raza Ahmad Khan, a judge special in a Court for Speedy Trials, an Islamic court. In 1979, General Zia al-Haq introduced Islamic justice into modern Pakistan as part of his attempt to balance growing Islamic nationalism against his military dictatorship. Called *Hudood* law, this Islamic justice system makes robbery (called *haraba* by followers of *Hudood* law in Pakistan) a crime that can be punished by amputation. The Boyds are the first foreigners to be tried and convicted under *Hudood* law.

The trial lasted two weeks, with testimony that left the brothers confident. "Our lawyers shattered the prosecutor," says Daniel about the proceedings. "We were free in our minds." That's when the judge laughed and the Boyds were found guilty by him of all the charges against them. As the amputation sentence was announced in the courtroom, Daniel yelled, "This isn't an Islamic court! It's a court of infidels!" As the brothers were led back to Peshawar Central Prison, Sabrina Boyd looked at her husband and said, "We keep praying all the time. A Muslim should never lose hope in Allah's benevolence."

They appealed the conviction and sentence to the Pakistani Supreme Court. Although the *Hudood* has been on the government's books since

|||||||||||||||||||||||| The Boyd brothers, with Charles's wife, Debra, in the Peshawar court where the judge sentenced them to amputation. Their hands and feet were saved by an appeals court judge. (Photo: AP/World Wide Photos)

1979, and although others before the Boyds have been convicted under it and sentenced to suffer amputations for their crimes, no hands or feet have been officially cut off. All amputation sentences have been over-turned after appeals. There is serious controversy within Pakistan— among lawyers, theologians, and politicians—about the use of the *Hudood.*

Some of the debate is technical. There are Islamic scholars, for exam-ple, who disputed the sentence because it called for the cutting of the Boyds' right hands. They claimed that the Koran mandates the loss of the left hand for theft. Opponents of the Boyds' sentence also insisted that the Koran never calls for the loss of a hand for a first robbery offense and never calls for the amputation of feet for robbery. The judge claimed the feet must go because the crime was so serious. Others question any interpretation of Islam that would include carrying out amputations in the modern world.

The *Frontier Post* editorialized against executing the sentence be-cause of the potential political consequences. "Since the convicted per-sons in Peshawar are American citizens," the paper pointed out, "the government should be prepared for an onslaught from the U.S. Con-gress and the myriad of human-rights organisations inside and outside Pakistan. The goodwill the government had earned internationally through its policies of liberalisation will soon evaporate as the interna-tional press goes on the rampage against the Peshawar verdict. Let us all hope the sentence is remitted in the appellate court and the country doesn't have to go through another trauma."*

Yet back home, as the brothers waited for their case to travel through the appeal process, their mother's lobbying at the State Department to help her sons seemed to be going nowhere. "We've all heard stories," she says about the lack of help she feels she received from her own govern-ment during her family's crisis. "Now I've lived it."

Patricia Saddler tells of frustration, of meeting with representatives of the State Department who invoked the Privacy Act and refused to dis-cuss her sons' case. At that point, she decided her only avenue of attack

---

*The *Frontier Post* displays this Koranic quote on its masthead: "And cover not Truth with Falsehood nor conceal the Truth when ye know." The "other trauma" the paper referred to was the amputation sentence years before against a boy who stole from a mosque. Hundreds of thousands of letters came from all over the world to General Zia and the Pakistan press just before a scheduled Zia trip to America. Zia delayed the sentence in an attempt to save his reputation during the trip, and then overturned the punishment once he returned to Pakistan.

was publicity. She works for a lawyer, and together they drew up a press release. It detailed the arrest and announced the brothers' claim of innocence.

"The two brothers," says the release, "maintain not only their innocence, they also maintain that they did not receive a fair trial. It is the brothers' position that police officers lied about where the weapon allegedly used during the robbery was found. Ballistics tests were not performed for three months after the robbery although the police had the weapon allegedly used in the robbery within days. According to Daniel Boyd's wife, an alleged confession obtained from Daniel was signed while he was threatened with a gun. The alleged confession, according to Daniel's wife, contained statements not made by Daniel. The confession was written partially in English and partially in Urdu. Daniel does not read or write Urdu."

Among other complaints, the release argued that witnesses who picked the brothers out of a police lineup were told beforehand that the two were suspects, and that the same witnesses changed their descriptions of the robbers after viewing the brothers at the lineup.

As they look back on the whole experience, the Boyd family says it can find no evidence that the State Department helped free the Boyd brothers. As an example of the inefficiency of the U.S. government representatives, they point to the day the brothers were in court to hear the results of their appeal. A U.S. consular officer joined them in the courtroom and told them the situation was grim. If the government had been exerting appropriate pressure, reason the Boyds, the officer would have had a less negative assessment of their case.

They claim that the reports sent back to Washington by the consular officer who visited the brothers in jail were misleading, suggesting conditions for the two were much better than they really were.

But in response to an inquiry about the Boyds from Representative Stephen Solarz, Beth Jones, the chargé d'affaires in Islamabad, certainly makes it sound as if the U.S. government made some efforts for the Boyds. She writes that she and her colleagues are following the case very closely, and "We have sought to ensure that the Boyds have adequate legal representation and we have made quite clear our concern that the brothers are accorded appropriate and humane treatment and all rights under Pakistani law."

Then she suggests there might be less to worry about than the results of the trial indicate. "It is our understanding that no sentence of amputation has been carried out in Pakistan since the *Hadood* ordinances were passed in 1979." She tells Solarz that the embassy has, in fact, interceded in the justice system in regard to the threatened amputation. "We have made known our view that clemency should be extended to Charles and Daniel on that part of their sentence."

Finally, the letter to Solarz claims that the U.S. government was making efforts that may have been more valuable than the Boyds realized during the discouraging time they spent waiting through the appeal process. "Moreover, you can be sure that government officials in Pakistan share our concern about the effect that carrying out a sentence of amputation would have on relations between Pakistan and the U.S. and indeed on Pakistan's international reputation. I have personally conveyed our concerns on this matter to senior Pakistani government officials, and will continue my efforts on behalf of the Boyds."

But back home the Boyds' mother remains unconvinced, saying she doesn't know why she received so little help from the U.S. government. "The first time I was hurt by my government," she says, "is when Eisenhower lied about Francis Gary Powers. From that point on, I've been consistently disappointed by my government. It is inconceivable to me. I don't know why. It just boggles my mind. Do you really think we don't have Vietnam vets alive over there?"

Patricia Saddler is convinced that the press coverage of the case, along with some help from the few congressmen she called on, influenced the Supreme Court. "I really believe," she says, "had not the media and the congressmen got involved my boys would still be sitting there." As the three of them tell their story there is a tone that makes them sound as if they feel completely alone; victims of some sort of conspiracy against them from an evil Pakistan and an uncaring America. Perhaps it is an understandable response, considering the terror of their misadventure, a terror that they must all have felt no matter how strong and sincere their faith in Allah. Now they are in debt, jammed into Patricia's tiny Dupont Circle apartment, wondering what to do next.

The Boyd brothers aren't the only Americans to end up behind the bars of Pakistani prisons. The prison population there included a sizable complement of Americans in the late sixties and on through the seventies, when Pakistan was a stopover on the heavily traveled overland route from Europe to east Asia. American travelers, looking to save money or just looking for adventure, crowded Pakistan's highways and railroads.

The continuing war in Afghanistan and the Islamic revolution in Iran ended the popularity of overland travel through Pakistan, and when I passed through Karachi there was only one American cooling her heels in the filth of Karachi City Prison. She had refused to sign a Privacy Act waiver, so the U.S. authorities would only tell me about her, not her name. She wanted to serve out her sentence anonymously, so her mother back in New York would not find out about her heroin possession.

Substantially less than half of the Americans arrested abroad are picked up because of drug law violations. Nonetheless, thousands make the mistake of consuming or smuggling illegal drugs in the wrong places abroad. How do these Americans allow themselves to end up in such compromising positions, facing primitive jail conditions and extraordinarily oppressive penalties? Of course, many of them go looking for the trouble, seeking thrills and riches. But temptation often comes searching for the vulnerable traveler.

"Hello," says a friendly-looking man as I make my way down a crowded Karachi street. He approachs me as I am browsing among the sidewalk peddlers selling cassettes of wailing Pakistani music, fresh fruit, and rich nuts. "Can I help you? Are you looking for something?" he was a nice-looking old Pakistani man. "You want something to smoke?"

I politely decline.

"I got good stuff," he cajoles.

Americans stand out in a foreign crowd like the gullible outsiders too many turn out to be, great targets for persuasive hashish salesmen.

The U.S. consul in Karachi is anxious to talk, to tell me about what he considers a much too lenient average sentence meted out to Americans caught carrying small amounts of heroin. "We don't like that," he says speaking for his government. "We'd like to see that longer."

Those charged with violating the law in Pakistan face a civilian court or an Islamic court or—depending on the current political climate—a martial law court. The police agencies pressing the charges determine which court takes jurisdiction over the culprit. Civilian courts maintain a reputation for the least harsh treatment of defendants, who cannot post bail and remain free while waiting for their trial in any of the courts.

Echoing his colleague in Bangkok, the Karachi consul expresses no

sympathy for convicted Americans, and no interest in helping them beyond his legal obligations. "We're U.S. government representatives, not
the representatives of a particular family. The family looks at the embassy as a prisoner's advocate. That's not the case. We cannot give them
legal advice." Of course, when and if it is in the U.S. government's interest, embassies and all other relevant components of the government
do not hesitate to get involved in foreign affairs. "I might know the
judge," the consul unconvincingly tries to explain his hands-off policy.
"It's inappropriate for me to talk with him about the case."

Then, this time agreeing with the Tokyo American representative,
the Karachi consul minimizes the dreadful conditions inside Pakistani
jails. "I don't think I could handle D.C. city prison," he muses. "I think
I could handle a Pakistani jail. Bugs you're going to see," he acknowledges, while insisting, "but it's not a pig sty. It's not super clean.
The food is edible. You probably won't get dysentery in prison here.
Pakistani food is cooked food."

Then he sends me down the hall to meet with his assistant, assuring
me I should experience few problems getting permission to visit the City
Prison. *Arrogant* is one of the words jotted down in my notebook to describe the assistant. Her whole manner—body language and scathing
commentary—personifies disdain for the Americans she is assigned to
help. She sits behind her desk, insisting that Americans are treated just
fine in Pakistani prisons. On her office wall is a framed certificate from
the Drug Enforcement Administration thanking her for helping to control the drug traffic.

She epitomizes for me the inequity that exists for so many Americans
locked up overseas. Yes, they often are guilty of breaking laws and committing stupid and egregiously foul crimes. But I am finding myself
more and more offended that American officials like this consular officer
in Karachi feel so little, if any, empathy; they often even seem to show
satisfaction seeing their fellow citizens suffer.

"Pakistan is a society in transition," she says, defending the local culture against complaints from American women traveling through the
country. "As society becomes more and more Islamic, opportunities for
misunderstanding increase. Sex discrimination does happen; people
must be prepared for that. It would be foolhardy for a couple of teenage
girls to come bum around Pakistan. They would be asking for trouble."

With this said, she suggests it would take at least a week to get approval from the home secretary to gain access to the prison. My taxi driver teaches me otherwise.

First I stop by the offices of *Dawn*, the leading English-language newspaper in Pakistan. I suspect it covered the New Yorker's trial. In an alley next to a foul-smelling creek, I try to keep my breathing shallow as I climb the stairs up to *Dawn*'s antiquated offices. It is like stepping into newspaper history. No video display terminals in the newsroom, not even electric typewriters. No computer search facilities in the library, just huge scrapbooks filled with yellowing clippings from back issues. Breathing the aroma of newsprint and ink, under a slight breeze from the slow-turning overhead fans, I study the narcotics file.

I find nothing about the arrest and trial of an American woman, but discover one reporter is clearly assigned to the heroin beat. I meet with him later in the day and although he can't find his stories in the files either, or locate his notes about the case, he does remember the woman's name. The U.S. Privacy Act can do nothing to protect Americans from the Pakistani press or its open court sessions.

The next morning I leave the Intercontinental and walk past the taxis that operate in conjunction with the hotel. Just down the street the gypsy cabs wait for fares. I am looking for a free-lance guide who will not feel an allegiance to the hotel, who will be more open to making an unusual arrangement than the hotel taxi drivers.

I pick a man who is lounging around his battered old Toyota or Datsun. I know his English is pretty good because for the last couple of days he has been calling out to me as I passed, trying to get me to buy drugs.

We get to know each other a little better on the ride across town to Central Prison. Once I finally convince him that I really am not a potential customer for his heroin, he stops trying, smiles and pronounces me "an honest man." He teaches me one of his favorite sayings as he drives and judges me. "Five fingers . . . is not same." He holds up his hand explaining that although all hands have five fingers, all men are not the same.

We park near the prison, a crumbling, colonial remnant. The yellow stucco walls of the main building are surrounded by a courtyard. The dusty courtyard is filled with garbage blowing when there's a breeze, a breeze that only lifts the stench of rot. Machine-gun nests are in place, and goats wander around the yard. A crowd of people is pushing and shoving, yelling and gesturing at the medieval-looking iron main gate, the entrance to the prison. These frantic-sounding Pakistanis are trying to arrange a visit or just pass food past the guards to their friends and relatives inside. There is a small window in the gate, barred with mesh. From inside, prisoners push and yell at the visitors. Every few minutes somebody goes in or out, or bags of groceries are sent inside. Uniformed police stand around the yard marking time, playing with guns left by their colleagues who went inside on prison business.

My cab driver is enthusiastically in my employ now, eager to prove his mettle. He wants me to find the American woman. He's convinced an interview can be arranged. But at the prison gate, I'm told by the guard behind the wire mesh window the same thing I was told at the embassy, "Get a letter of permission from the home secretary."

"Back to the Intercontinental," I tell the driver dejectedly, and we start walking toward his car.

He smiles and laughs. "This is Pakistan. Everything costs money in Pakistan. Do you have money for the police?" I tell him money is not a problem.

"Then you can see her," my guide assures me. "We'll give the policemen some money. I know him," he says of the guard at the main gate. "I used to come here to visit a friend and bring him food and cigarettes."

So we head back toward the filthy, crumbling fortress, and in the yard I see evidence of money talking. I watch two prisoners being brought into Karachi Central. They're local, wearing long shirts, baggy pants, rags on their heads, and sandals. They are chained together, but with chains loose enough to allow them easily to shove wads of bills into the pocket of the guard escorting them to the iron gate.

The cab driver has me write my name and the woman prisoner's name on a scrap of paper. He pushes it toward the guard at the window in the gate. The word is that we'll have a chance for the visit later in the afternoon.

I spend a frustrating afternoon, waiting and watching in the yard. I study the machine guns up on the roof in the watch huts, the goats chewing on the garbage. Children run around. The faithful pray at the mosque in the yard.

The sun beats down hot as the hours pass. I keep asking the cab driver to check on what is happening, he keeps telling me to be patient. I have nothing else to do, so I wait and try to be patient. I watch the police playing with their guns, and guards with bayonets fixed on their rifles or carrying bamboo canes. I watch vendors peddling their disgusting-looking food and the dirty water they sell in plastic sacks. Periodically I join the mob at the gate and beseech the guard there about my visit until he shoos me away with the rest.

But finally, just as I am about to give up, I am sent to the visiting arena. It's an outdoor walled-in area alongside the main prison wall, with barred windows covered with wire mesh cut into those walls. The noise is deafening – reminiscent of Thailand – as Pakistanis yell back and forth to each other, pulling on holes and tears in the mesh to pass in money, cigarettes, and food to the prisoners.

I stand around with the bored goats, looking at the prisoners through the thick mesh, trying to find my American woman. Then the prisoners suddenly leave and a new group is ushered into the visiting cell. It is easy to spot the only Western-looking woman, despite her local garb. I think it is her eyes; they don't seem as accepting of her fate as the others. I make my usual rapid-fire speech to her about my intentions, explaining who I am and why I am visiting. As soon as I convince her that her name will not be used, she won't stop talking.

"It's no place for a woman to be, I'll tell you, especially for a foreigner." I push my little tape recorder toward her, coaxing, "Speak louder, speak louder." As she tells her horror stories about attempted rape and degrading living conditions, I eye the guard, but he looks unconcerned.

"The grounds are terrible. You see the grounds here," she motions to the goats, garbage, and dust behind me. "That's as bad as it is inside. Most of the time it's covered with water, so you have to walk through puddles."

She speaks fast and fiercely. "The food they serve you is beans and rice every day. If you have money, you can buy your own food. If you don't have money; forget it, baby. You starve to death." She paints a much different picture of the cuisine than what I heard about in the embassy. "Some of the food they serve you has worms in it. I mean, this is no place for an American. Your own type of food, you can't find it in this country."

She has enough money to pay friends to bring her food from outside. She gets potatoes and rice, bread, eggs, sometimes bananas, apples, and guava. Once in a while she receives some meat. "Otherwise I would have to probably eat this shit." When she was first incarcerated she ate the prison food. "You get diarrhea from eating beans all the time. You get a runny stomach. You have nausea constantly. You're throwing up. You get fever. Because the rice that they serve you here in prison isn't clean, you have to clean it yourself. It's half cooked; you have to cook the rest of it yourself. The beans have worms in them," she says again. "It's terrible."

She complains about the doctor and his medications, telling me some of the pills he dispenses cause sickness instead of curing it. "If you need an injection, don't get one. Die first!" she laughs a New York sarcastic street laugh. "He uses the same needle for every single person inside this place." She pauses for a second. "It's a terrible life."

The Islamic culture just adds to the problems of prison life, she yells. "It is screwed up. The whole system here is, forget it. If I go outside my gate, I have to be dressed [in traditional Islamic-style clothing]. That means I can't wear my jeans. They won't let me. Because all the men will start staring at me and start touching you and everything. If it wasn't for the fact that I have a husband, I would probably be raped by now."

She says she was molested on one of her trips between the prison and the courthouse. "I almost got raped in the Black Maria, the police van that takes you back and forth." I ask her what happened, and the response is from the New York streets again. "I knocked the shit out of the guy, plain and simple. He went to grab me. He tried to rip my clothes. He tried to rape me in the Maria and I just knocked him out because I'm American. I don't take no shit, you know? I'm American. I've been in America all my life, you know? I live in New York City. So I know how to handle people like them. So I just beat him up in the Maria, plain and simple."

This is a confident woman, convinced she is going to get through her six months in Karachi City. She describes her small room with a hole in the floor for a toilet, a hole that periodically stuffs up. She rooms with two other women.

"The guards here are okay. If you want something desperately, you have to bribe them with money and you'll get anything you want. Like if you want them to send a message to someone and they don't want to send it, you give them money and they'll send your message. The only reason why I get my messages where they're supposed to go is because I'm American." She believes that if the U.S. consul did not visit periodically, and if good relations with the United States weren't so important to the Pakistani government, she would be treated just like the rest of the prison population. "Left alone to die," is how she puts it.

Not that she's happy with her relationship with the U.S. authorities. "The only thing they're doing for me is sending me books once a month.

Other than that, I tell her something and it just goes in one ear and out the other. I ask her to do things for me; they're not helping me at all." I suggest that maybe the U.S. consular officers are only doing the bare minimum for her because she was caught smuggling heroin. "That could be a possibility," she acknowledges, "but there's still no excuse for it because I'm still a human being, just like anybody else. You know, I make mistakes. Everybody makes mistakes. I'm sure the consul has made dozens of mistakes."

So what's the daily routine, as she sits out her sentence in the squalor of Karachi City Prison? "I try to think of nice things, but most of the time all you hear is the people who are sick here in pain. You really can't think much. Most of the time I sit and cry." The tough New York facade wanes for a moment, or she's seeking sympathy. But I doubt it. Despite the institutionalized skepticism of so many of the U.S. authorities, I don't think the prisoners I interviewed, like this woman, lie much, if at all. They may embellish a story here and there, but even that I question. I look around at the grime and rubbish. I look into the dark visiting cell and listen to the sounds of the other prisoners and their visitors. I imagine that were I to be locked up in one of these foreign hellholes, I too would shed some tears.

"Most of the time I sit here and I cry. You know, it's terrible. I try to think of nice things. But then when you think of the nice things, you end up being miserable. I've lost, like, fifteen pounds here already, just sitting and thinking and wondering when am I going to come out."

She's glad for an opportunity to offer advice. "If you come to Pakistan, for people who want to travel, it's nice. Don't get in the business of heroin, because you're going to get in jail. Just like me. They have ways of finding out everything you do."

We say good-bye and she disappears, back into the bleak, noisy prison, half a world away from home.

Videotape in Saudi Arabia, Jailbreak in Iran

> What I'd really like to say is that if the president is not going to answer any questions, I damn sure am not going to answer any questions.
>
> General Norman Schwarzkopf, speaking to reporters at the White House after the Gulf War

> In Saudi Arabia, you're guilty until you're proven guilty, and you'll stay in prison until they kick you out the door.
>
> Texan George Creagor, upon his return home from Damman Central Prison

|||||||||||||||||||||| **A**t the end of the complicated visa form for travel into Saudi Arabia is a simple declaration that the applicant must sign. "I hereby certify the above statements to be true to the best of my knowledge and that during my stay in Saudi Arabia I shall abide by the laws and all regulations of the Kingdom." More than a few careless Americans signed that promise and failed to live up it, either because they didn't bother learning those laws and regulations or because they believed – incorrectly – that they could get away with bending the Kingdom's strict codes.

"At the moment of arrest I was sitting in my home, just like this, watching television with my wife and young son." Like so many of the Americans working in Saudi Arabia, petroleum engineer Al Levine speaks with a soft Texas drawl. "There was a knock on the door, and then six soldiers with submachine guns are standing over you. They put two of them over my wife; scared her to death, of course." Levine was initially picked up on pornography charges.

From the freedom and safety of his Houston home, Levine ridicules the charges. "You have to understand that over there pornography is not what we mean by pornography. Pornography over there is a father kissing his daughter in public. Right now," he points to a woman, "the way you're dressed, in your short sleeves and your ankles showing, you are considered evil, wicked. You must understand, every Western woman is considered a whore and prostitute. By definition. By the religious definition. And the religious definition is the national definition. So it's very difficult for a person like me and others who have been held over there to get across what we're really talking about."

A movie rated X in America, *Last Tango in Paris,* is the first example to come to Levine's mind. It is banned in Saudi Arabia. But what angers Levine is the hypocrisy he sees in the Saudi culture, hypocrisy that he misinterpreted. "For example, the Moslem religion absolutely forbids alcohol; the manufacture, the consumption, or anything else of it. You're told that here." Levine was one of the thousands of Americans who take advantage of money-making opportunities in the Saudi oil industry. "But when you go there, you find it in unlimited supplies. But everybody pretends like it doesn't exist."

There are no liquor stores in the Kingdom. "But," says Levine with disgust, "if you want a hundred gallons of alcohol, believe me, you can get it tomorrow morning. Or if you want one gallon. It's a little bit of a shock, particularly the first time you get there, you heard all of this propaganda given to you over here, and you get there, and it's completely reversed."

When the police interrogations first started, Levine was confident that he'd be freed quickly. "I'm totally convinced that at any moment the American consul is going to come in with a hundred marines and save me, because that's what it says on TV. I know I haven't done anything and I know there's some kind of mistake here and I realize that any minute now everybody's going to forgive and forget and I'm going to go back and go to work."

As the interrogators continued their work, Levine slowly started to realize that a different scenario was unfolding. "The interrogator is across the desk and without warning he opens a drawer and pulls out a Time-Life book. He slams it on the desk." The book is about Israel and the world's religions. "He says, 'We've taken this out of your house.'

I don't doubt that for a second. I buy a lot of books." Levine says he recognized the book just as his persecutor announced, "This is a terrible book."

But the prisoner still didn't understand the problem. Was he being questioned about the propriety of owning the book? Finally, the policeman "flips this book open to the front and the introduction. He points his finger down to the bottom of the page and right there it says, 'Editor, Robert Levine.' He says, 'That's your relative.' You have to understand what's going on in my mind. I can't imagine what he's talking about."

As the hours-long interrogation continued, Levine was accused of running a wife-swapping club in Saudi Arabia and smuggling blue movies into the country. The police suggested that in addition to coordinating the expatriate swinging scene in Dammam, Levine was videotaping the action. He claims there is no truth to any of the charges and that as best he can reconstruct the case, an unknown informant—for reasons Levine insists remain a mystery to him—called the police and made the accusations. "That, I think, is what started this whole thing." The result was a four-year prison sentence and a fifteen-thousand-dollar fine for possessing and distributing obscene videotapes.

Levine says the police confiscated his personal videotape library as evidence. "Every videotape," Levine says about his supposedly pornographic collection, "came through Saudi customs. How do you get them in? They come through the mail or they come through the airport customs. Certainly nobody's idiotic enough to carry a triple X; if they are they're insane. No, you carry everything from Walt Disney to anything that you see on American TV. We have friends over here recording it in the United States and they mail it to you. It gets over there and there's a big red stamp on it, Opened by Saudi Censor."

Levine says he was convinced he had done nothing to violate the law and that the police found no evidence of any wrongdoing. But during all this time—the initial investigation lasted three weeks—Levine was locked up and, he says, periodically beaten. "They wake you up by kicking you." After three weeks he was kicked awake and taken into an office where his wife was sitting. "The interrogator said, 'Do not look at her. Do not blink. Do not raise your eyes.' I was in handcuffs, unshaved; I looked like I was in a concentration camp, I'd lost weight already. He says, 'You tell her to confess.'"

Levine says his wife was scared, but said nothing. "I give the little girl credit. She gave her name, rank, and serial number, and that's all she'd say to those people. She was scared to death of them, because she knew more than I knew. She knew that the American consul wasn't going to do anything. But I didn't know this; I had had no contact with any outsider. So she knew that anything she said could hurt me. So she wouldn't say anything."

Her silence, he says, infuriated the guards. They told him to order her to confess. She still refused and she was led from the room. At that point, says Levine, the chief interrogator told him that if he did not confess to the charges levied against him, his wife would be arrested and put into prison. Convinced that they would carry out their threat, and that she would suffer interminably in a Saudi jail, Levine broke. "What did I confess to? I confessed to being a member of a video club." Levine maintains that most of the expatriate oil workers also were members, that thousands of videotapes were traded back and forth by foreigners working in the oil fields to help fight the boredom of desert duty. "It's no secret. I confessed I was a member of a video club. Yeah, it was true, I was a member of video club, never have denied it. Still don't deny it." But he disputes the validity of his confession to the pornography charges. "That thing was given under duress. It was because I was scared, frightened, mentally blown apart, and particularly because of my wife. I didn't confess. I signed that blasted piece of paper because I had to."

In the safety of Houston, wrapped in the protection of the First Amendment, admitting to be a member of a video club sounds absurdly inconsequential. But there was nothing frivolous about his confession there in Saudi Arabia. He was then taken from the interrogation cells, where he says he had been beaten on the kidneys with a rubber baton and on the soles of his feet with a wooden stick, to an ordinary prison. There, for the first time, he saw the American consul and says the message from the U.S. official was not to expect that his government could do anything to help him out of Saudi custody.

He was stunned, and his Texas attitude started to show. "I said, 'You guys are not doing anything. You're letting this country, this Saudi zero culture, push the United States government around. You're not protecting me in any way. You're not doing anything. What is this? Why don't you protest?' " Levine feels the American officials assumed that he was guilty, just because he was behind bars. "Their attitude is one of lofty disdain," he says with disgust, remembering the time when he and his cellmates broke out in an all-body rash and the U.S. officials refused to bring needed medication.

He describes a U.S. and Saudi policy based on hypocrisy and deceit; Saudis drinking with Americans in a country where liquor is forbidden, American politicians overlooking Saudi human rights abuses because of the strategic importance of the Kingdom. Levine, and many of his colleagues who had difficulties with Saudi authorities during their tours of work duty in Arabia, charge that this duplicity leads American contract workers to believe that it is all right to violate Saudi laws and customs, as long as the drinking, dancing, swimming in bikinis, and the like are private activities engaged in behind closed doors or on the oil company compounds where the foreigners live and work. "It's illegal, but you do it anyway. You're exempt," is how Levine sums up the recreational routines of the Americans and other foreigners. That's probably how he rationalized including some tapes that could be considered pornographic in his collection. He acknowledges owning some such tapes, but insists he never lent or rented them to others.

For the next sixteen months, Levine sat in an overcrowded cell. He says he was never beaten again, but experienced other types of abuse. "The food is horrible. Do you eat it? Of course you eat it, you get so hungry." The lights were never turned off; one ceiling fan stirred the air. In the cold winter there was no heat; in the summer the cell became an oven. After three months, he finally saw a courtroom. "I was sentenced in Arabic, with no translators. I get a year. This trial takes place in about two minutes. You don't have any defense." He spits the words out, his Texas accent emphasizing the first syllable of *de*fense. "There's no accuser standing there. Months later, I'm taken back and told that the case has been reviewed in Riyadh and I'm sentenced to four years. I'm ready to commit suicide. Four years. You can't play dominoes, you can't play cards, you can't play chess. You can't do anything. It literally fries your brain."

Levine says he finally managed to bribe his way out of prison. "Every year the King is merciful and releases everybody from prison. Quote unquote. The trouble is, he doesn't release everybody from prison. He releases some. What they say and what they do are two different things. I was told if I paid my fine I could be released." He paid up, packed his bags on the scheduled release date, and walked up to the prison gate. "I'm standing at the door that walks out to freedom and a Saudi walks up to me and says, 'We're not letting you loose yet. We've added an additional fine.' I'm scheduled to go get on the airplane in two hours."

Two weeks later his wife had scraped up the additional eight thousand dollars. "Finally, they handcuff you, walk you to the airplane in handcuffs, take your handcuffs off and try to kiss you, and put you on an airplane."

From Texas, he sums up his Saudi experience with venom. "I went over there with the belief that I was doing right. I was arrested. I was abandoned. My career was destroyed, is destroyed. My health is perhaps destroyed. And I don't expect justice. I just want simple revenge."

Al Levine's story is just one man's story, of course. Is he telling the truth? A better question is, why would he lie? And his credibility increases dramatically because there are so many similar stories told by other American contract workers who find themselves locked up in Saudi jails, charging that they've been abused by the Saudis and abandoned by the American government. Dallas petroleum engineer Bruce Munden is another example. He came home after eight months in a Saudi prison telling stories of being strung up on a rack for punishment, seeing the bloody footprints of other American prisoners whose feet had been beaten raw, and expressing no appreciation for the work of the American consul. "They didn't give a damn," he says bitterly. "They are not responsible for my release. They had the least amount to do with it. They won't stand up for a citizen's rights."

Thirty-five years old when he got home to Texas, Munden was no neophyte to the complex workings of the Saudi oil industry. He and his company had been doing business in the Kingdom for over six years when he became involved in a contract dispute with his Saudi partners. They complained to the authorities that he owed them money. That was all the police needed to hear. By Saudi law, a simple business disagreement is enough reason for the police to lock up a foreigner pending the resolution of the dispute, even if no criminal charges are filed and no law is broken. This device was used in Munden's case, the Saudis told him, because he was an American and they wanted to ensure that he didn't leave the country.

He claims his Saudi partners were involved in a scheme to defraud investors and wanted Munden out of the way while they carried out their plans. Once they split up the take, "they went their own separate ways and there was no one around to tell the local police that there was really no reason to hold me. So I was held for eight and a half months because no one came forward to say, 'Turn him loose.' "

The prison conditions appalled Munden, who calls them, "a step above a zoo. You get up and leave your cell and you walk back to the communal toilet; you have to literally bathe and use the toilet in the same open hole in the ground. You turn the water on to take a shower and all of this comes floating up around your feet. So you're bathing in a cesspool. It's an old, antiquated block building that has no air conditioning. The only windows are just slits at the top of the walls that are so high you can't get up to them. There's no heat or air conditioning. It does get very cold in the winter in Saudi Arabia. In the summer it got to 127 degrees and a hundred percent humidity because you're right on the coast in Dhahran. So people break out to the point where their bodies are just a solid sore from the perspiration and the heat."

What Munden can't understand is why the U.S. authorities in Saudi Arabia didn't demand better conditions for the Americans. "The State Department is not willing to admit that these things are going on. They say, 'No, there is no abuse,' and 'No, there is no torture,' and 'Yes, they're being treated all right.' In fact, you have thirty-two Americans who have been beaten beyond belief. They get up out of their bunks to walk to the toilet and their feet crack open and leave bloody tracks all the way to the toilet. So who do you believe? Do you believe the State Department? Or do you believe the Americans who come home with scars emotionally and physically from what's been done to them?"

Munden was locked up over a month before he saw an American consul. "My friends informed the consulate within twenty-four hours of my arrest, so they knew I was there." Munden says he was left unattended so long because, "at that point the consulate officers that were serving the prison and visiting the prisoners literally considered it the lowest duty at the consulate to have to make the periodic trips to the prison." He says he was told, "You're the last on our list of priorities. If we get everything else done, we'll come look at you all or see what's going on here. But you got here of your own accord; it's your own responsibility. You knew the risk when you came to this country and we're obligated to come visit you, but that's all we're obligated to do."

For Munden and his fellow prisoners it was a harsh lesson in reality. And as his months behind the walls dragged on, he became more frustrated with his government. "The British consulate, the New Zealand consulate, we would see them come and visit prisoners. They would bring them food, they would bring them vitamins, they would arrange special privileges for them. But the American consulate never offered, and when asked refused to do anything for the American prisoners there."

Finally, after friends in Texas organized a letter-writing campaign, the charges against Munden were dropped and he came home, still frustrated by his own government's response to his complaints. The State Department answered a letter of inquiry from Texas Senator Lloyd Bentsen with the familiar refrain, "We are continuing to work with the Saudi authorities to resolve some of the problems raised [by Munden] and to insure that American prisoners receive adequate food and proper medical care. We cannot, however, demand that U.S. citizen prisoners be given preferential treatment or rights not accorded nationals of other countries."

The State Department letter rejected Munden's other charges as well. "With regard to Mr. Munden's allegations that the Consulate General is ineffective because of the officers assigned there, we can find no evidence to indicate that any of the officers assigned to the Consulate in Dhahran do not effectively perform their duties. In fact, as Mr. Munden is probably aware, it was the direct intervention by a vice-consul with the local sponsor which resulted in Mr. Munden's ultimate departure from the Kingdom of Saudi Arabia."*

Munden came home lobbying for change, insisting that the U.S. government should do more to help Americans locked up overseas. He refuses to accept the argument that the State Department is forced to sacrifice the needs of individual Americans because of more important national security goals. Before his Saudi prison experience he accepted the claim that there are delicate problems in foreign policy that the average American can't understand. He came home with a different message. "The State Department is just as ineffective as the U.S. Postal Service. They have no more integrity and no more expertise. There's nothing magical about what they do." Get rid of the career Milquetoasts in the State Department and replace them with a tough stance toward foreign governments is Munden's recipe for improvement.

My requests for a visa to Saudi Arabia to tour Saudi prisons and interview Americans in custody were rejected repeatedly. "What's in it for

---

*The May 8, 1984, letter to Bentsen was from W. Tapley Bennett, Jr., who was then Assistant Secretary for Legislative and Intergovernmental Affairs.

us?" asked the Saudi ambassador in Washington, suggesting that I first investigate the condition of Palestinians held in American prisons.

As for Bruce Munden, he says he's learned his lesson well: "I will never willingly set foot in a Middle Eastern country again."

During the Gulf War, many Americans toured the Middle East as part of the military operation. The U.S. authorities made formal attempts to teach the Americans how to avoid violating local laws. The USS *Wisconsin*, for example, printed its own guidebook when the ship allowed sailors liberty in Dubai, one of the United Arab Emirates.* The book warned

If you haven't heard yet, the U.A.E. follows the Islamic religion. Alcohol (booze, beer, wine, etc.) are forbidden by the Islamic religion. Police in Dubai, as in most Islamic nations, are REALLY hard line on public drunkenness. In Dubai, unruly, intoxicated people WILL be picked up by the police and JAILED for a MINIMUM of 10 days! So don't get "boozed," you could end up in a really HOT slammer! The cabbies will also "clip" drunks for a higher fare because if the drunk doesn't pay, the cabbie just takes him to jail. If you are arrested, chances are they will "throw your misbegotten hide" in a very unpleasant "calaboose" and there you will rot.

But even after the United States fought a mercenary war to supposedly protect Saudi Arabia and its oil fields, Americans in Saudi prisons continued to be denied basic internationally accepted rights. In its "Report to Congress on Americans Incarcerated Abroad" for 1991, the year of the Gulf War, the State Department Bureau of Consular Affairs complains about Saudi Arabia again: "The problems described in the 1990 report concerning delays by Saudi officials in notifying the U.S. Embassy about the arrest of a U.S. citizen persist." The explanation for those delays is unsatisfactory, especially given the close postwar relations of the two governments. "Saudi law enforcement authorities do not immediately inform U.S. consular officials about the arrest of a U.S. citizen. Instead, they notify the person's sponsor, who is usually the em-

---

*My favorite lines in the USS *Wisconsin International Bon Vivant's Guide to Dubai, United Arab Emirates* are: "Don't be all shocked and bothered if you see two Arab men holding hands, kissing, etc. This is a sign of friendship or of greeting. It doesn't have the same meaning here as it would if it happened in San Francisco."

ployer. The sponsor, or a family member, then reports the arrest to the Embassy. Saudi officials in time inform the U. S. consular officials about the arrest of a U.S. citizen."

But timely notification of an arrest is not the only problem facing Americans in Saudi prisons, acknowledges the official report. "Beyond chronic notification problems," it continues, "prison visits are difficult and time-consuming to arrange. Permission to visit a prisoner, which must be obtained through the ministry of foreign affairs, takes about a week to secure." The State Department insists it's working on the problem. "Our Embassy and two consulates general continue to press and, as in the case of consular visits to prisoners under military jurisdiction, to negotiate for less complicated, less time-consuming procedures to visit prisoners."

What Munden and Levine couldn't understand – and this was before the Gulf War – was the passive approach the United States took toward Saudi violations of international standards in regard to prisoners. After the Gulf War, after the United States came rushing to answer the Saudis' call for help, it is even more difficult to understand why visitation and notification problems persist. Certainly the U.S. government is in a position to demand to see its nationals, not just "negotiate."

Another Texan, businessman and 1992 presidential aspirant H. Ross Perot, shares Munden's and Levine's disdain for the role the U.S. government plays when Americans get in trouble overseas.

In the midst of the 1979 Iranian revolution that overthrew the Shah and installed the Ayatollah Khomeini, a mob of armed civilians stormed the Gasre Central Prison in Teheran. Some eleven thousand prisoners escaped that February 11, as the crowd tore open the prison and the guards scattered. Among the freed were common criminals, political prisoners, and myriad unfortunates detained on a variety of charges, but not yet tried, including a few Americans.

A United Press International reporter was in front of Gasre as the prisoners poured out, some coming over the walls, others through the main gates, still others out windows past bars they managed to bend apart. One of them was Mary Ellen Schneider from Bethesda, Maryland. "I'm trembling," she told the UPI reporter, "I feel like a nervous wreck." Schneider was a linguistics professor at Teheran University until a man fell off the roof of her apartment house. Then she was arrested, held for suspicion of complicity in the fall, and spent almost two years in Gasre. "People from the outside came to our cell and literally dragged us out," she described her rescue. "My jewelry, passport, everything I have except this bundle of clothes, is inside there. I'm trembling all over. I can't think. But it feels good."

A few days later, Perot took credit for the jailbreak. He explained that he orchestrated the attack on the prison to rescue two American inmates, employees of his Electronic Data Systems Corporation who were being held on business corruption charges. At a Dallas news conference Perot insisted that the mob outside Gasre was incited by his commandos, who paid Iranian revolutionaries to fire up a crowd and attack the prison. "We first confirmed that our government could not do anything to help our men," Perot said at the conference. "We then arranged with revolutionary leaders in Iran to have the prison mobbed."

The escape story is told in the Ken Follet book *On Wings of Eagles.* Follet, in his preface, finds it necessary to write, "This is not a 'fictionalization' or a 'nonfiction novel.' I have not invented anything. What you are about to read is what really happened." His caveat was likely prompted by the skepticism that greeted Perot's claims at the news conference. In the book, Follet identifies an Iranian employee of Perot's company—called by the pseudonym Rashid—as spontaneously deciding that he could convince the frustrated Iranians in the streets to turn on the prison.

"The people in there are prisoners of the regime," Follet quotes Rashid as shouting in the streets. "If we are against the regime we should let them out!" Rashid led a growing band toward Gasre, writes Follet, and in front of the prison made another speech: "The jails must be taken over by the people, just like the police stations and the garrisons; this is our responsibility. There are people in Gasre Prison who are guilty of nothing. They are just like us—our brothers, our cousins. Like us, they only want their freedom. But they were braver than we, for they demanded their freedom while the Shah was here, and they were thrown in jail for it. Now we shall let them out!"

Rashid, according to Follet, broke into the prison and—in the midst of the confusion he generated—into a guardroom, found cell keys, and passed them out to the crowd with the cry, "Open every cell—let the people go!" Among the prisoners who escaped that day were Paul Chiapparone and William Gaylord, the Perot employees.

Years later, Perot speaks of the episode with pride to a colleague of mine. "They kept our two people as insurance that we would come back after the revolution was over and start up the computers again. Nobody had ever said they had done anything wrong; they didn't accuse them of anything, just put them in jail. We went through the State Department; I had access to everybody in our government. We tried all the channels; we hired Iranian lawyers. They wanted a 12.75 million-dollar bond at one time. They wanted it in an Iranian bank. We got it all the way to Kuwait. But the banks were closed because of the revolution, and you literally couldn't get it from the Kuwait branch of Bank Omran into the Teheran branch of Bank Omran. In the meantime, the Shah was leaving the country, Khomeini was coming into the country." Perot talks fast. "They were killing people right and left. We had two people who were innocent just locked up in a prison. And we had a basic decision to make, either leave them—and they would have died or been killed—or rescue them. We made the decision to rescue them."

That Perot organized a team to try to rescue Chiapparone and Gaylord is clear. Whether his man Rashid is responsible for the assault on Gasre Prison is less clear. Immediately after Perot's Dallas news conference, State Department officials pointed out that Gasre was only one of many Iranian prisons stormed by revolutionary mobs. But Perot maintains he called off his commando attack operation when he saw how well fortified the prison was, and decided instead to buy a mob to do the job.

Not that Perot is promoting such rescues for Americans with friends, family, or co-workers locked up overseas. "It was a very specialized circumstance," he says, "and nobody should generalize from that experience. First off, unless you have the ability to do it, you don't want to try it." Perot had the money to finance a rescue, and he hired a professional to lead it: Arthur Simmons, a retired Green Beret who was in charge of the 1970 unsuccessful raid on a North Vietnamese prisoner-of-war camp at Son Tay. "And secondly," says Perot, "you want to be very careful. I don't recommend it. The first thing I said when we came home is, 'We're not going to do that again.' "

But whatever the exact details of the escape may be, Perot's assessment of the value of the U.S. government is unequivocal. "Don't count on the government to do anything. An American overseas is on his own. Anybody that thinks anything else than that just doesn't understand the system. The State Department is very weak to the point of being nonexistent in terms of representing Americans effectively overseas."

The advice that escape is a last resort is echoed by lawyer Richard Atkins and his colleague from the International Legal Defense Counsel, Robert Pisani, in their 1982 booklet, *The Hassle of Your Life*. The lawyers working within the ILDC specialize in dealing with Americans locked up abroad.

You may want to consider trying to buy out a relative or colleague, suggest Atkins and Pisani, or arranging an escape. "However, these procedures are extremely dangerous, and while many individuals incarcerated abroad may seriously consider one or more of these alternatives, their use is fraught with danger for your relative, yourself, and any representatives participating in such a venture. While buying your relative out and arranging for his escape are frequently talked about, especially in prison circles, they very rarely, if ever, succeed. Buying your relative out, for example, almost never succeeds once he or she has been formally charged and papers have been drawn up on his or her case." Atkins and Pisani really hammer the point home: "Escape à la *Midnight Express*, while making exciting movies, rarely succeeds, and in fact a number of Americans have died attempting to escape from foreign jails."

But prisoners do escape, and the U.S. government official policy toward escapees, as stated in the *Foreign Affairs Manual*, is fascinating. Consular officers are told to report any escapes to headquarters in Washington immediately. But the instructions continue, "A U.S. citizen who has escaped from the place of incarceration is still eligible for the full range of consular services, provided there has been no request from the local authorities to deny such services." According to the State Department, a new passport and a loan to get home are the two most common requests from escapees.

If the escapee is not wanted by the United States, then a new passport can be issued. "The consular officer should make it clear," advises the manual, "that documentation does not guarantee that the escapee will exit the host country, and that the post cannot assist the escapee to evade local authorities after leaving the post." Not only that, if the local government has asked to be notified if the prisoner comes looking for new papers, then the U.S. authorities overseas are instructed by Washington to inform local authorities if the prisoner is equipped with a new passport.

So, under just the right circumstances, the U.S. government will help a American running from trouble overseas to get home.

Credit Cards and Bibles

> Marvellous things happen to one in Greece—
> marvellous *good* things which can happen to one
> nowhere else on earth. Somehow, almost as if He
> were nodding, Greece still remains under the pro-
> tection of the Creator. Men may go about their
> puny, ineffectual bedevilment, even in Greece, but
> God's magic is still at work and, no matter what the
> race of men may do or try to do, Greece is still a
> sacred precinct—and my belief is it will remain so
> until the end of time.
>
> Henry Miller, *The Colossus of Maroussi,* 1942

> Man is a prisoner who has no right to open the
> door of his prison and run away. A man should
> wait, and not take his own life until God sum-
> mons him.
>
> Socrates, quoted by Plato in *Phaedo*

|||||||||||||||||||||||||| I wouldn't go back to Greece again!" John Jay Bonstingl is adamant as he remembers the details of his nightmare in paradise. Several years after his encounter with the Greek criminal justice system, the memory of his disrupted vacation is fresh and clear. In the mid-eighties, Bonstingl was a high-school social studies teacher and a bachelor. He enjoyed spending the long holidays away from school seeing the world. "I was a well-traveled man by the time I went to Greece."

He was well enough traveled to feel comfortable going to Greece in the summer of 1985. That was just after TWA Flight 847 had been hijacked. President Reagan responded to the hijacking by advising Americans to "review the wisdom" of flying to Greece. Pan Am took his advice and canceled its daily flight to Athens, and the switchboards at travel agencies lit up with cancellations of Greek and European vacations. Americans in record numbers stayed home for the summer holidays because of the growing national fear of terrorist attacks on Americans and American targets.

Bonstingl was unruffled, "I've always been a bit adventurous, so I didn't even think twice about it." Then he corrects himself. "Yes, I thought twice about it because of the State Department advisory." The State Department warned Americans to stay away from the Athens airport because security there did not meet U.S. government standards. "I took that under advisement and I thought, 'Nah, nothing will happen.' Well, the airport was fine; it turned out to be other parts of Greece that were not so fine for me."

So in July, Bonstingl headed off for a cruise of the Greek islands. In fact, the terrorism scare added to his hopes for a satisfying trip; he looked forward to seeing Greece without as many competing tourists as usual. On the last day of the cruise, the boat stopped at Santorin for a couple of hours of sightseeing and shopping. The tour operators told the boatload of tourists that this was the ideal spot to buy gold jewelry; it was not too expensive and the craftsmanship was excellent. "I took out my Visa card and I went looking for a shop."

Bonstingl's tale at this point sounds like the stories told by many travelers shopping abroad with dollars. "I was walking along and this young gentleman beckoned me into the shop saying, 'You want some gold? Here's the place!' He spoke perfect English. I walked in, I looked around. I'm not a good shopper. I like to buy what appeals to me and then go. I saw a couple of gold chains that I thought would be terrific. They were really quite pretty and I thought they'd be good investments." Bonstingl bargained with the shopkeeper, and was happy with the final price. "I walked out of the shop after giving him my Visa card. I signed the chit and chatted with him a bit."

During their conversation, Bonstingl pointed to his cruise ship down in the harbor and told the merchant that he was island-hopping as one of its passengers. "I left and both of us were smiling."

That was the last port of call. The next morning the ship was back in Piraeus early and Bonstingl was still sleeping when the ship's loudspeakers barked out his name, asking him to report to the office. He threw on some clothes and made his way to the front desk and found the purser. The purser was holding a telex and Bonstingl suddenly feared his sick mother or elderly aunt back in the States had died.

"I said, 'What's the news?'

"He looked at it, he looked at me, and said, 'You bought some gold yesterday.'

"I said, 'Yeah.'

"He said, 'And you used your credit card, your Visa card?'

"I said, 'Yes.'

"He said, 'And you knew it was no good and you bought it anyway and these three men are here to take you away.' "

Three plainclothes, armed policemen were waiting. They took him back to his cabin and allowed him to pack, with their guns out, pointed at him. Off the ship, they piled into an unmarked car and drove him off without telling him where they were headed. He had been shown no identification; Bonstingl was wondering if the three men were really even policemen.

One thing Bonstingl was sure of, as the car careened toward the jail that would be his home for the next few days, was that he had purchased the gold in good faith, with a valid Visa card and no intent to defraud either the merchant or the credit card company. He was convinced that he was not even over his credit limit. As it turned out, he was a few hundred dollars over his two-thousand-dollar limit, because bills from a spring trip to the Soviet Union were still trickling in to his account. The bills had not arrived before he left home, so he had not yet paid them.

This is a scenario that occurs regularly for frequent travelers. The only way to avoid such a situation is to keep a running tabulation of exactly how much is charged against any one account and then—once the account limit is reached—not charge more until the bills clear and are paid. Few credit-card users in America subscribe to such a policy, and indeed, the whole system of credit buying is structured to encourage just the opposite; credit card companies enjoy the income that they make from the extraordinarily high interest rates.

Travelers usually do not make arrangements to pay bills that arrive during their absence. Consequently, it is not uncommon for a credit-card bill with months-old charges finally posted to show up, skewing a traveler's credit expectations.

It is not only tardy postings, like Bonstingl's Soviet charges, that cause credit-card debts to exceed a customer's credit limit. When a traveler rents a car or takes a room at a hotel, the car rental company or the hotel often interferes – usually without the customer's knowledge – with the credit that is available on the credit-card account. If a room in a hotel costs one hundred dollars, a hotel will typically put through a hold on a customer's credit for two hundred dollars, expecting that the traveler may order some expensive champagne from room service, or might stay another night. This hold is not billed against the account. But the hotel, in concert with the credit-card company, sets this credit aside in case the customer runs up charges that exceed the basic room rate. Car rental companies do the same thing, in case the renters keep the car for longer than originally reserved.

Although this system may protect merchants, it can ruin travel plans. A hotel reservation of several days or a contract for a few weeks of car rental can wipe out a credit-card balance, making further charges impossible, or even illegal.

For John Jay Bonstingl, the next stop was the port police station. The station was not open yet, so the four of them waited out front for the chief to come and open it up for business. "When I got inside, they put me on the line with the U.S. embassy. They told me that what I had done, or allegedly had done, in the U.S. was nothing at all but in Greece it was called a crime against the state." Specifically he was being charged with check fraud. The logic was that Visa, and other similar cards that were issued in Greece at the time, were not issued as credit cards. They were debit cards, which drew directly from bank balances. So going over a limit didn't just add to a high-interest consumer debt, it was the equivalent of overdrawing a bank account. The fact that the terms of a Visa card were different when the account was issued by an American bank did not matter to the Greek authorities.

Bonstingl learned all this on the telephone at the Piraeus port police station. In shock, he heard the embassy employee on the other end of the line tell him that he was in very big trouble. "Good thing I hadn't seen *Midnight Express.*"

From the police station, Bonstingl was taken to the Piraeus holding cell. But before he was locked up, the police took him, under guard, downtown and allowed him to telephone America. He called a friend in Maryland and arranged for Visa to increase the credit limit of his account to cover the gold chains.

"It was a common cell," Bonstingl says about his accommodations for the three days following his frantic call to America. "I heard the door slam—now I know why they call it the slammer—this heavy iron clang resounded in back of me, just a couple of inches in back of me." He's dramatic as he describes the scene, but then he has that liberty. One day he's a happy-go-lucky tourist buying local trinkets and souvenirs, the next day he's locked up without a hint of when he'll be free again. "I peered into this room filled with the most ghastly human beings I'd ever seen in my life. A small group of them crouched in a circle, a cigarette dangling from an Al Pacino-like young man, from his mouth. They looked at me in silence for a couple of seconds and then they just burst out laughing. It was such an anomaly in my life; there was no way that I could bring myself to realize that this was reality."

Before Bonstingl could decide how to react, "Al Pacino" gestured for him to come over to the group. "I didn't know whether to go or not. I mean, what do you do? What do you do in a situation like that? It's such an incredibly foreign circumstance. Not the least of which was that I didn't speak any Greek."

Bonstingl made his way toward the group and "Pacino" came over to him, "bellowing in Greek. I told him in English, 'I don't understand any Greek.' I'm not sure if I was petrified at that point or so filled with the illusory quality of this whole experience that I was numb. I'm not sure."

But, as is usually the case in such an encounter, the two started communicating. They used a few common words and hand gestures. The man wanted to know why Bonstingl was in jail. Bonstingl showed his Visa card "like Karl Malden. He looked at it, his eyes bugged out, he slapped his head with both hands and made motions to me saying, 'You're in jail forever.' "

In fact, Bonstingl faced a maximum of twelve years in prison for his crime. One of his cellmates had just been sentenced to eight years of hard labor for the same offense. For the next three days he sat, and paced, and gained a new respect for his wretched colleagues in the tank.

"The custom in Greece," Bonstingl learned, "even among criminals is that you don't mistreat a guest." Since he was the last to arrive and a foreigner, he was considered the guest. Nonetheless, he bribed a guard to allow him to use an adjacent private cell after his convict hosts "made attempts to steal everything I had with me, including my watch." Apparently a little larceny didn't violate their sense of hospitality.

His new home was a "small, dank cell with no ventilation, half the floor a lake of urine. But at least it was away from these," he gropes for a second looking for the right word, "these animals." He says he felt threatened the whole time he was locked up.

As is so often the case in foreign prisons, the toilets were holes in the floor, flushed with a spigot. Food came from a café across the street. "Indigestible," Bonstingl calls it. Instead of eating, he lost fifteen pounds during his ordeal.

Three days later he was taken by ferryboat, again under armed guard, back to the island. The next morning, the man who had sold him the gold showed up yelling, "You tried to cheat me, you tried to cheat me!" Bonstingl told him to try to put the transaction through again. He did. By this time his credit limit had been raised and the gold chain purchase cleared the Visa account. The merchant dropped charges and Bonstingl was presented with a paper to sign—in Greek. As he looked over the paper, the phone rang. It was the U.S. embassy in Athens checking on his status. He asked if he should sign the unknown paper. "Sign that and just get the hell out," was the advice from the other end of the line.

Bonstingl likes to tell the anticlimax to his story. He had lost his luggage during his days in jail. The Santorin jailer pinched and slapped his cheeks, he stumbled out into the village, and made his way into a store to buy a duffel bag for what was left of his possessions. The clerk told him she only had one bag left. "She reached up on the shelf," says Bonstingl with satisfaction, "and she said, 'This is the only one we have left. Will this do?' I unrolled it, a black and red Nike duffel bag, red handle, red trim. Big bold red letters across the front said, America Is Number One."

Bonstingl says his traumatic days behind Greek bars do not deter him from traveling, but he's intent on never returning to Greece. "I wouldn't go back to Greece again because of the experience I had there." But he insists that's not the only reason. "You know, some places you go in the world, you like to go back. Some places you just don't find an affinity with the surroundings or with the culture. I found much less affinity with the people of Greece than I had expected."

Once home, Bonstingl found he'd lost some of his affinity for his Visa card, too. "These days I try to leave home without it," he likes to say with an irritated laugh, mixing his credit-card advertising references. He filed suit against Visa and his Maryland bank, seeking forty-two million dollars. He claimed that they should have warned him about the danger of using his card in Greece. The federal courts took just a few minutes to

‖‖‖‖‖‖‖‖‖‖‖‖‖‖‖‖‖ Educator John Jay Bonstingl back in the States after his un-scheduled week in a Greek jail. He still travels, but not to Greece. (Photo: Courtesy of John Jay Bonstingl)

throw his case out, making it clear yet again that the onus for an American's security overseas rests ultimately on the traveler's good sense.

Don Stephens says he was shocked and amazed at the sentence he received from a Greek court. "We didn't think that giving a Bible, a New Testament, would ever be a criminal offense." In fact, he did not even know the Greek authorities were after him until he was safely out of the country. "I felt like I took a five-hundred-year step back into the Middle Ages," he says about the charges brought against him for proselytizing. "I didn't have any idea that we could be accused of a criminal offense." But he decided to return to Athens to face the music and make a point.

Stephens is a Christian missionary and president of Mercy Ships, an organization based in Linden, Texas, that operates three ships around the world providing free medical help. Along the way, they teach their religion to whoever listens. In the early eighties, one of those who listened was a sixteen-year-old boy in the Greek town of Mégara named Costas Cotoupolon. At the time his parents were involved in an especially acrimonious divorce, and young Costas told his story to Stephens and other crew members of the *M.V. Anastasis.* "So we prayed with him," says Stephens, "told him that he could turn to God in situations like this and pray for restoration of the relationship with the mother and even if the divorce was never turned around he could still learn through these difficult situations." Then Stephens and his group gave the boy a copy of the New Testament, the version called the *Living Bible,* written in modern Greek and in an updated style.

The gift, Stephens thinks, made the mother irate because the father had introduced the boy to the missionaries. She sought and received a restraining order forbidding the boy from making any more contacts with the religious organization. Shortly after that court decision, the *Anastasis* sailed from Greece and proceeded with its charitable work.

Two years later, Stephens was telephoned by a Greek friend and informed that he and two colleagues were being charged in Greece for the criminal offense of proselytizing. "I think proselytism is a word that's a little offensive here," said Stephens at the time of the court case, "because all we did is the open exchange of ideas and the giving away of a New Testament. He does," Stephens described Costas, "have a deep personal belief in God and is reading his New Testament and surely that shouldn't be a crime in any nation today."

Stephens returned to Greece to stand trial, charged – along with his

Greek and British colleagues—with violating a law passed during the Metaxo dictatorship that ruled Greece in 1938 and 1939. "My father strongly imbedded in us a sense of ethics. That's my understanding of Christianity. You do the right thing." The law he was accused of violating restricted open discussion of religion that did not agree with the traditions of the Orthodox church. Stephens says he actually sympathizes with the rationalization for the law against proselytizing. "I understand the law was based on the history of Ottoman rule in Greece when proselytizing was by the sword; change or die. I abhor that. I believe in the free exchange of ideas." And he believes in the value of the ancient translations of the Bible used by the Orthodox church. "I understand the necessity of revering old documents. But when modern Greek has changed so much it is hard to understand—it would be like reading medieval English. We didn't know this modern Greek translation would be a problem."

Probably not, but there were many factors at work as Stephens's case moved slowly through the Greek criminal justice system. Of course, arguments about the interpretation and translation of the word of God historically have fueled much worse than court cases. But in addition to the religious issues at stake, it seems a vengeful mother was using the courts against her son and former husband. Stephens, who says, "I went back because you do what's right, not what's convenient," and his organization received extensive and positive worldwide publicity from the case. "Well over two million people signed petitions that were delivered to Greek embassies around the world," he remembers years later. He believes the government was looking for publicity, too. "It was more political than it was religious," he says of the case and the trial. "The Papandreou government was in power. He was anti-American at every opportunity. I don't think the Orthodox church had anything to do with it. We have too good relations with the Orthodox church."

Just before Christmas in 1984, Stephens and the others were found guilty of both the proselytism charge and the attempted abduction of young Costas. Stephens finds the attempted abduction charge particularly ridiculous, saying Costas had wanted to sail with the ship, but was turned away because he was not old enough to satisfy the group's criteria for volunteers. The sentence meted out to the defendants was three and a half years in prison.

The three men appealed the decision to a higher court, and were allowed to remain free on their own recognizance pending the results.

Eighteen months later the appeal was heard and Stephens headed back to Greece saying he was willing to accept the prison time if the appeal was denied. "We're willing to face that," he said, "not joyfully. We certainly don't anticipate spending some time in a Greek prison, but I think that these issues are primary issues, and we must be willing to stand and face the consequences if we're going to fight for basic human rights and freedoms. I think that is what has made America unique and different, and we have to be willing to assist those in other nations who want those same freedoms."

Stephens saw his case as an important opportunity for his missionary work. "Even had we known that we could end up in prison for distribution of the New Testament, we probably would have done it. I cannot see why this book is so feared. Perhaps there is the power in it that darkness doesn't like to know about. We find in all repressive regimes a hatred for the Bible, Old and New Testament together."

As it turned out, Stephens and the others never served time in prison. After five days of appeals court proceedings, the higher court prosecutor recommended that all charges be dropped, and the judge so ruled. But the repressive Greek law against proselytizing remains on the books.

Baptist minister Michael Birks leads a rural congregation in northwest Oregon these days, convinced that he's a better preacher because of his time in a Czechoslovakian prison. He, like Stephens, was persecuted because of his evangelistic activities.

Birks took a break from college in 1979 to make his first trip to Europe, a working vacation as a volunteer for the Slavic Gospel Association.* He was assigned to make contact with Christians living under Communist governments in Yugoslavia, Romania, Hungary, and Czechoslovakia and bring them Bibles and other Christian literature.

On July 3, he and two partners left Vienna for Slovakia. It's fascinating that thirteen years later he remembers the dates and other details of his prison encounter as if they had just occurred, a trait he shares with most Americans who are locked up overseas; the intensity of the experience is lasting. In their Volkswagen van were three suitcases jammed with Bibles and other religious books. "They weren't specially

---

*The Slavic Gospel Association is based in Wheaton, Illinois. There it trains missionaries like Birks for overseas assignments. In personal meetings and by means of a worldwide network of radio stations, the association evangelizes people who speak Slavic languages.

||||||||||||||||||||||||| Despite his conviction in Greece for proselytizing, Don Stephens managed to avoid serving any time behind bars. (Photo: Mercy Ships)

hidden," he remembers. At the Mikulov border crossing, the Czechoslovakian border guards came out to inspect the car. They opened the
suitcases and found the Bibles.

"They took us inside," says Birks, "and started asking us questions
about where we got them and where we were taking them." Meanwhile,
other guards were unpacking the suitcases, tabulating the books, taking
the side panels off the interior of the van, and removing the seats, looking
for more contraband. They found nothing of interest to them beyond
the three suitcases of books.

After about five hours in the border station, other interrogators arrived and asked Birks and his colleagues, "Did you know it was ruining
our economy to bring these into Czechoslovakia?" The Slavic Gospel
Association and their volunteer workers realized there was some risk
shipping boxes of Bibles into countries governed by authoritarian and
oppressive regimes, but they always insisted that nothing in Czechoslovakian law prohibited carrying such religious literature into the country. "As far as we knew," said Birks later, "no Americans had ever been
arrested and we thought it was legal to bring Bibles in because Bibles
were printed in Czechoslovakia, too." Apparently the inspectors were
interpreting their own laws in the same literal manner. Birks was never
told he violated any law because his baggage included Bibles. Instead,
the inspectors informed the three young students that they were being
arrested for "attempting to bring undeclared articles across the border."

They were shipped to Brno, separated from each other, and locked
up in an old stone prison. For the next five and a half weeks, Birks was
kept twenty-four hours a day in a small cell with two Czechoslovakians
who spoke no English. Birks had not studied either Czech or Slovakian.
The cell was equipped with a toilet and a sink. Twice during his imprisonment he was allowed out to shower. He enjoyed no English-
language reading material, did not encounter the American authorities
until a few days before his release, and was unaware of the legal status
of his case or of when he might be freed. During his time in prison, he
never saw his colleagues.

"I paced my cell," he says, "taught English to my cellmates a little bit,
did a lot of praying and a lot of thinking."

Conditions were severe, but there was no abuse. The cell walls and
floor were concrete. The door was equipped with a peephole; there was
a small window and no bars. "If a guard saw you look out, he banged
his stick on the door and told you to stop." But Birks managed some

glimpses and saw the heavy barbed-wire fence that surrounded the prison wall and the farm country beyond.

He and his cellmates ("they might have been informers") kept the cell clean. Periodically it was searched by the guards. "It was a real eye-opening experience for a twenty-one-year-old who had never had a parking ticket."

As the weeks passed, Birks lost weight, coming out of the prison thirty-five pounds lighter. Breakfast was coffee and "a hunk of bread." Lunch was "usually a dumpling-type thing" and soup. For dinner the prisoners received half a potato and milk, sometimes some soup. "The soup," says Birks, "there were bits of meat in it. I didn't want to look at it. It was a real question what parts of an animal were in that soup. But overall," he accepts, "the food was okay. There just wasn't an overabundance." Twice during his confinement, dinner was topped off with a treat of macaroni noodles covered with sugar and unsweetened chocolate.

After ten days inside, "They told me we were being held for interrogation and that until we told them the name and place where we got the Bibles and where we were going with them, we would never get out." He told them nothing. His two partners kept quiet, too. "I figured we had a better chance of getting out as Americans than he would have," Birks says of the contact to whom he was assigned to deliver the books. "We told them," he recalls with pleasure, "it would be a long time before we talked, that there wouldn't be any reason to say anything."

The Czechoslovakian government kept quiet, too. They did not, contrary to the norm of international relations, inform the American government about the three prisoners. Meanwhile, the Slavic Gospel Association knew something was wrong because the three had failed to show up at their planned Slovakian destination. Pressure was exerted on the U.S. embassies in Vienna and Prague to conduct a search. Finally the Czechoslovakian authorities acknowledged that they were holding the prisoners, and an American consular officer visited Birks on August 3 — a month after he was first locked up — and told him the U.S. government hoped to convince the Czechoslovakians to expel the three evangelists.

Back home in California, Birks's parents waited patiently. "I'm quite concerned about it because it has been a while," his mother told the San Francisco *Examiner*, "but the Lord has to look over it, because I can't seem to help." At that point there was no indication that the U.S. government was much help either. "We haven't been given any promises at all," Marilyn Birks said. "The State Department said from their past experiences, the detention is like in a hotel room, not a prison."

Four days after his visit from the American consul, Michael Birks and his two friends were taken to the border, given their personal possessions, and told to walk back to Austria. The border guards kept the Slavic Gospel Association's old VW and the seven hundred Bibles and other books. Birks credits his release to a combination of prayer, the efforts of the U.S. government, and worry within the Czechoslovakian regime about its image in the world community. "The three things together, that's what got us out. But more than anything," he's pleased to believe, "it was the Christians around the world who were praying for us." Still a puzzle to him after all these years is why no U.S. authorities met him and the others when they finally were released from prison.

Thinking back on his experience, Birks is convinced it was good for him and that he was aware of its value while he was in prison. "There were times," he acknowledges, "when I kind of wondered why I was there. Here I was trying to help Christians behind the iron curtain. But the more I got to reason through that, I realized maybe I can help them by experiencing a little of what they go through on a regular basis. I knew I'd get out." And now, with the radical changes in government there, he hopes to go back and see Czechoslovakia again.

"Primarily, I grew a lot as a Christian at that time. I had never been challenged. I probably grew more in those weeks – as far as faith – than I had in the previous five years." He says he was told he came back a changed man. "I can't really quantify it. I probably came back a lot more grown up, a lot more sure of myself."

He sees another benefit to his incarceration in the publicity surrounding his case: a consciousness-raising about conditions in Eastern European countries under Communism. "It provided an opportunity for people in American churches to realize that people behind the iron curtain really did suffer, that a lot of people do pay a price for their faith. So it was beneficial, not just for me, but for other people."

Happy to discuss those old days, balding and bearded, Birks keeps talking. "I guess if I'd known I'd spend time in prison I wouldn't have gone," he says about his summer trip. He pauses to make sure the point he is about to make is not missed. "But I wouldn't trade for anything the time I spent in prison and the Christians I met behind the iron curtain."

He smiles. "I'm probably more committed than a lot of other people because of it."

Once the iron curtain became a fading memory, more Americans started traveling in the looser atmosphere of Eastern Europe, and encounters with the law increased. In early 1992, for example, an American expatriate named Chris was picked up by the Prague police and charged with theft and fraud. He was held in Ruzyně jail on the outskirts of Prague while his case was investigated, giving him the dubious distinction of being one of the handful of Americans known to be held in prison in post-Communist Czechoslovakia, and one of the few Americans locked away in the former Communist Eastern Europe.

Ruzyně is where prisoners from Prague and its environs await trial or other presentencing proceedings; convicted inmates are sent to different institutions after their days in court are concluded. Randall Lyman, a reporter for the English-language Prague newspaper *Prognosis*, describes his visit to the jail to see the American prisoner.

The guards were friendly, jovial; one even found a chair for me for the waiting room. None spoke English. The few prisoners I saw looked healthy, full-faced, not emaciated. I saw a group out on the street in some kind of light work brigade. Uniform like pictures of the Gulag: thick blue work pants, padded jackets with padded tubes for sleeves, shaped to armor rather than clothe the body.

Ruzyně lies in an outlying district of Prague with the same name, near the famous White Mountain where in 1620 the rebellious Czech Protestants got slaughtered by the Catholic Hapsburg armies. A lot of open fields in this part of town, some of it agricultural. The city feels exposed here, underdeveloped, open against the wilds; this area lay far outside the walls and battlements of old Prague; it was incorporated into the city only in the 1970s.

Immediately around the jail, there's a counterpoint between the seeming construction that's going on behind aged and weathered scaffolding, and the decay of old, neglected buildings. Half the local traffic is trucks. Rough outcroppings of gritty, eroded brick protrude from the sides of walls where some other wall was torn away. A stripped and smashed up bus sits outside the gate, beneath empty watchtowers and barbed wire, its gut lying in fragments on what used to be the floor. Even a moderate wind kicks up the storms of dirt from the streets.

Inside the prison grounds, the place retains the feel of being half-abandoned, half-under-construction as I walk along the unfinished concrete walkway leading from the entrance to the building where I'll meet Chris. Because it's winter, there's only dirt and a glaze of snow on the ground. At intervals along the jail's outside wall are small white signs that read *Vstup Zakáz*—entrance forbidden.

Inside the building where I meet Chris, the corridors on the lower floor are barred off from the elevator lobby by gates with peeled and chipped paint the same old-eggshell color as the walls. This is not a building, but a steel crate. The elevator holds three people, and if one of them is fat, it's hard to close or open the doors, which open inward. And if he smells too, like the officer who rode up with me, you're glad this thing doesn't go higher than six floors.

This is a far different Prague from the quaint, ancient city familiar to hordes of tourists since the 1989 revolution dismissed the oppressive Communist government and swept Václav Havel and his reformers into the presidential castle. A "horrible place," Chris calls his jail, saying, "the accommodations are a step above horrendous." From his perspective, the Velvet Revolution has not yet reached Ruzyně. He says he was beaten by police the day he was arrested and led to believe that if he signed a paper he could not read, he would soon be out of trouble. The paper was a confession.

Chris describes the policeman in charge of extricating the confession as "this scum, he was really a scum-of-the-earth-type police detective. Big fat stomach. You know, he spoke broken English. And he was just like everything you would read about in a Communist country." Chris signed the confession, "and he said, 'Oh, no problem for you, no problem.' And then I never saw him again."

Instead he encountered another investigator who looked at the signed confession and said, according to Chris: big problem, big problem. "So, you're being mind-fucked, as well as everything else, as well as the physical torture, the physical pain that you feel from the beating. They're screwing with your mind." Later, U.S. diplomats acknowledged the beating and the impotence of the U.S. government to prevent most such abuses at the hands of arresting police, even in a nation so allied with America and so solicitous of favorable world opinion as post-Communist Czechoslovakia.

Chris was judged temporarily insane at the time of the crime. Since he had returned the stolen goods, he was freed after spending a few months in Ruzyně.

Accidentally Smuggling Antiquities out of Izmir and Other Turkish Adventures

> Shopping is one of the great pleasures of a trip to
> Turkey. Most visitors to Turkey cannot resist buy-
> ing at least one or two things. Your only likely
> difficulty shopping in Turkey will be in deciding
> what to choose from the many hundreds of tempt-
> ing bargains.
>
> From the tourist brochure "Turkey,"
> published by the Turkish Ministry of
> Culture and Tourism and distributed into
> hotel rooms throughout the country

|||||||||||||||||||| **B**arry Crandall speaks in staccato bursts of incomplete sentences. We're sitting in a pizza restaurant in the Nevada desert. He's working as a welder now, and without too much prodding looks back to his wandering days. "Okay. What happened was." He stops and starts over. "I can go back to the hippie days. Hippie. San Francisco. Sixty-five, six, seven. The whole Buddhist thing, we're going to India. At twenty-one I inherited X amount of money; it was enough to take me there. So I went. Barcelona, Spain, first. Boat to Istanbul, which is the beginning of the Hashish Trail. The only drugs I was on were mari-juana, LSD, hashish. No hard drugs. Got to Istanbul, lived in a real in-expensive place. Ten cents a night. Lived up there, everything was mellow. I was going to Kathmandu, Nepal."

Crandall was not alone. There was a crowd of young Americans on the Hashish Trail back then. Many of them were staying at his cheap Istanbul hotel. "One night the police came in. I'm an American, they can't bust me. They busted me. They came in, they took my pack apart. I had my dope, which was less than one ounce of hashish." He remembers it well, "Lebanese hashish," he specifies. "They busted me. They loaded nine of us into a jeep convoy scene, went down to the police station. This was 1968. They told us, 'This is a routine case. You plead guilty. You sign your name to the guilty plea and then we'll kick you out of the country and that's it.' So we sign all the papers and then they go, 'Ha!' Immediately after that we were in the biggest prison in Istanbul."

It was at that prison a few hours later—strip-searched and head shaved—that Crandall asked the first Westerner he encountered when he should expect his deportation. The sobering answer was two and a half years, minimum. "I got a lawyer. I wanted to arrange bail to get out of this prison. Just over three months later, he got me out on bail. I got out."

Once out of jail, Crandall jumped bail for Greece and came home. "I look back on it as a real good experience; I wouldn't have missed it for the world." Suddenly the words are coming faster as he insists that his months locked up in Turkey were an important coming-of-age opportunity. "I learned things about human nature that I could never find anywhere else. It was a valuable experience; I would do it any day because I learned. I was a spoiled-rotten rich kid and I got thrown into this thing and I learned what it was all about. The whole thing."

The escape from Turkey took Crandall a few months to plan and accomplish. "I got out of prison and my lawyer and everybody in the know told me I had to get out of the country." His advisers were adamant about this because they were convinced that once Crandall was tried, he would be found guilty and returned to prison. He does not include his own country's representatives as among those who offered him advice. "The American embassy just wanted to disown me. They didn't want any part of me," he says with disgust these many years later.

While Crandall was locked up he had befriended a Canadian prisoner with a severe mental disorder; he fed him, clothed him, and cleaned him. The Canadian was completely unable to care for himself and was released from prison before Crandall managed to get out. "He was my charge, it was something to do. He was a nice person." Once Crandall was back on the streets of Istanbul, he checked in with the British embassy, seeking information on the status of his Canadian friend.

The British diplomat who sat down with him asked Crandall to share the details of his own case, and he, too, joined the chorus recommending that he flee Turkey. Crandall remembers the encounter fondly. "He said, 'Off the record, there is a train that goes from here and at one point it skirts Greece and you can jump out there.' I thought that was really risky because that border is well patrolled."

So Crandall bided his time, collecting information. "I was scared." And he was right to be afraid. If he was caught trying to escape, he expected his eventual prison sentence to be doubled. "If I could get to anywhere in Greece I would be free. I went to Izmir and on to the coast town Çeşme." Crandall stayed in Çeşme for two weeks, "trying to ingratiate myself, to find out how to get to Khíos because I'm an excellent swimmer." The Greek island is just over six miles from the Turkish coast. "I stayed up and watched the border boats. I was hanging out there. I had really short hair. I was trying to get loaded because the pressure was so incredible. I was alone."

After studying the coast and the Aegean, Crandall determined swimming would be too difficult and, with money wired from his parents in San Francisco, he bought a rowboat. His new plan was to sail to freedom. He tried to act the part of a tourist as he made his rounds in Çeşme. When he rented a room and was asked for his passport, he complained that it was lost. But he was growing paranoid, convinced the locals were wondering just what his real story might be.

The night before he intended to make a break for Khíos in his new boat, he met two other foreigners "with long hair," and together – along with a few Çeşme locals – they went out to the countryside to smoke hashish. "We're out in a field getting loaded," remembers Crandall, and one of the Turks told him "all the locals knew I had gotten out of prison and was trying to get out of the country. And the law knew."

So Crandall abandoned his boat and headed back to Istanbul on a coastal passenger ship, intent on discovering a new escape route. On board the ship he confided in a fellow passenger, who suggested Crandall take the same ship back out of Istanbul to Izmir because its route took it on to another Greek island, Rhodes. Just stay on board until you get to Greece, was the other passenger's advice.

Instead, Crandall encountered two more foreigners in Istanbul. They, too, were awaiting trial on hashish possession charges and the three of them decided to return to Çeşme, steal a fishing boat, and make a break for Khíos. But back on the coast, Crandall chose not to join his new partners as they pushed off for Greece because he felt the water was

||||||||||||||||||||||||| Before *Midnight Express* brought the horrors of Turkish prison home to Americans, Barry Crandall and his fellow foreign prisoners clown for the camera inside their Istanbul jail. For Barry (front row, far left), the memories are fond ones. (Photo: Courtesy of Barry Crandall)

too rough, the wind too strong and blowing in the wrong direction. He was correct. They crashed into rocks and swam back to Turkey.

By this time Crandall was getting advice from his lawyer to speed up his exit, that time was running out before his trial. So from Istanbul, Crandall boarded the ferry that stopped at Izmir and continued on to Rhodes. "I got on the boat, bought a ticket to Izmir." He could only buy a domestic ticket without a passport. "I was just thinking: this is a bust because when we leave Izmir, we're going to get searched."

But Izmir turned out to be no problem. "I walked right through customs. It was like I was invisible. It was unheard of—me, a foreigner. I got on. We left." As the ship headed south, he made the aquaintance of a honeymooning couple from San Francisco. Together they spent the night out on the deck, acting like tourists. Crandall was never asked to show a ticket. "The next day between Marmaris and Rhodes, I figured I'd just jump overboard and swim." But before he went into the water Turkish police boarded the ship for a search. "I was invisible again," he marvels, "I was just sitting there, taking in the sun like everybody else, and nobody asked me anything."

As the ship dropped anchor at Rhodes to transfer passengers onto a landing launch, Crandall faced still another obstacle. He needed a pass for the launch, but he couldn't ask for one because he was a stowaway. His new honeymooning friends came through. They passed up their own opportunity to tour Rhodes and gave him the necessary pass. "Far fucking out, Buddha is with me," he says he thought as he finally reached Greek territory. "It was the happiest I've ever been in my life."

Crandall calls his escape "the most harrowing time" of his whole Turkish experience. As he tells the story it seems remarkable to me, too, that he encountered no complications when he finally decided to make his break. To what did he attribute the successful operation, I ask him, an inefficient Turkish bureaucracy? Or might the Turkish authorities have decided to let him slip out of the country to save them the need to bother with still another American? There is a pause before he answers. "I never thought of it." Another pause. "It was probably both," he starts to say and then changes his mind. "If they knew it was me, it's not like the Turks to do that. They like to rub salt in your wounds whenever they can." He thinks some more and concludes, "It was my karma. I don't know why. I just had it smooth."

That Crandall was able to bail out after just a few months, and then escape Turkey altogether, must influence his positive memories of

Turkish prison. But he seems to be a hardened survivor who quickly figured out how to stay out of trouble in the prison. "My friends got whupped real bad," he says, "but not to where they couldn't stand it. They weren't crippled or anything like that, just something that you expect. You know, you get caught smoking dope in the joint, you expect to get whupped. Well, they got whupped. That's part of the routine. But on a day-to-day level, hey, it was just get up in the morning, put your bedroll away. You go down, you buy a little breakfast. They had people coming around, you know, vendors that had these incredibly beautiful breakfast foods. They were just delicacies to me. If I would have had them in the States, I would have just," he licks his chops and says, "Yum. Two cents, a kuru, two kuru. Warm in the morning. We had milk. Beautiful warm milk."

It is an odd conversation. Billiard balls are clashing near us in the pizza bar as Crandall warms up to his fond recollections, insisting the horrors of *Midnight Express* escaped him during his Turkish prison stay. He talks about the fun of outdoor volleyball games, expresses some irritation with the discrimination he felt from some of the Turkish prisoners, and sloughs off the whacks on the head he received waiting in the canteen line as just an understandable irritation that comes with prison routine. "We had the best coffee I ever had in the world, the best tea I've ever had in the world. We had music, we had dancing. I would rather be there than here, in a joint."

Crandall's assessment would be shared by Yil Maz Çelik, who was the warden at Buca Prison in Izmir, where New Yorker Gene LePere was held. LePere was charged with trying to smuggle an antiquity out of Turkey. She was visiting the Pamakkale ruins and bought what she thought was a crude Roman reproduction from an insistent souvenir hawker. "It's not true that all the prisons are so bad in Turkey," Çelik tells me in the bar of a hotel along the sparkling seashore in Izmir. He is no longer warden, but has been promoted to prosecuting attorney. "They are the same as the prisons in Europe," he insists.

"All the reports about miserable Turkish prisons are just propaganda," he says with satisfaction. We are talking through an interpreter. "You are asking about conditions in Turkish prison because of *Midnight Express?*" asks Çelik. The book and movie about Billy Hayes's arrest for hashish smuggling at the Istanbul airport, his imprisonment and subsequent escape, are famous in Turkey. The movie is banned when I visit Izmir, but bootleg videotapes are passed around among the curious.

I tell him that I am looking into the conditions faced by Americans all over the world, not just in Turkey. The interpreter translates. Çelik speaks again, and despite the thick Turkish accent, I can pick out the name William Hayes. "William Hayes escaped," says Çelik, "and then he got in touch with the Turkish authorities through his lawyer, saying, 'If the Turkish government forgives me, I will tell the truth that the Turkish prisons are not so bad, they are comfortable.' " Even if something is lost in the translation, it's difficult to imagine Billy Hayes ever offering to tell the world that the book and movie depicting his prison life so thoroughly misrepresented reality.

But Çelik isn't through. He says, "The Turkish government answered that we can't forgive him because a law was broken." Then he insists that Hayes was held in the most comfortable Turkish prison, "not a bad place, a good place. The prisons in the United States," he acknowledges, "are a little more comfortable than the prisons in Turkey, but the prisons in Turkey are not bad. The prisoners," he says seriously, "can live."

He talks about the decent food with the same enthusiasm as Barry Crandall, and the availability of television, daily newspapers, and books. So if conditions are so "comfortable," I ask Çelik, why do Americans maintain such a negative picture of Turkish prisons? Again he blames "William Hayes and misadvertising."

We talk about the LePere case next, and I explain how unreasonable it seems that LePere was arrested at all, not to mention how unjust her incarceration during the investigation of charges against her appears to Americans. Çelik's response is quick: "This can be in every part of the world. They found something in her bag. They tried to investigate it and she has to be in the prison during that time. This happens in every part of the world." He is convinced LePere was treated well, pleased to remember that LePere was not handcuffed in court.

"It is not true," Çelik says about the portrayal of Turkish prisons in *Midnight Express*. "It is a hundred percent normal that if a person does something against the law, he has to be in a prison. William Hayes did something wrong and he went to prison." What about beatings, the filth? "Lies, lies, lies," says Çelik.

"I wouldn't want to spend any time there," the American consul at Izmir says about Turkish prisons, calling Buca overcrowded and governed by what he terms "hard-nosed discipline. Not that I'm aware of that much beating. Strong discipline. You're not fed well, but you get a reasonable diet."

He's well acquainted with the two famous cases of Americans who passed through the Turkish criminal justice system. "Our impression is very clearly that they try to give foreign prisoners a better shake — vitamins, cigarettes, money, newspapers." He calls the law that Gene LePere tripped over "very vague and imprecise," and says the American authorities are working to have signs posted at archaeological excavations explaining that removing antiquities without approval is against the law. "Even if you buy a rug," he warns, "get a certificate that this is a modern rug."

As for Billy Hayes, "he was smuggling drugs." The American consul is matter-of-fact. "Turks do not like drugs. I think Turkish justice is fair. It is strict. Perhaps its biggest problem is the length of time it takes from the time of arrest to the time of final decision." As I travel around the world, from Thailand to Pakistan, and now here in Turkey, it is troubling to hear repeatedly from so many American prisoners that they feel let down by the efforts of their consuls. It is perhaps even more disconcerting to hear remarks like those of the consul in Izmir endorsing a justice system where prisoners are kept in substandard accommodations for barbaric lengths of time and beaten.

"If it doesn't affect you, you don't think about it." Years after his escape, safe in his apartment in New York, Billy Hayes still thinks about it. "I was the same, I was sure that I'll never get arrested. I'm just too smart, I'll never get caught." Hayes is sure too many world-traveling young Americans still are convinced it will never happen to them. The statistics that show that each year over ten thousand Americans can expect to encounter trouble with the law overseas back up his hunch.

He tries to tell anyone who will listen that they ought to be aware of foreign laws before they travel. "I tell them, do what you like and know what you're doing. Learn by experience; in this case somebody else's is better than your own. You can get busted. You can spend a lot of time in jail — not just drugs, we're talking about a lot of different laws in foreign countries that aren't the same as here. You find out the hard way you can go to jail for something you don't even know is a crime. When you're arrested for it, you say, 'Gee, I'm sorry, I didn't realize that.' And they say, 'Fine, but you are arrested.'"

Hayes isn't just concerned with naive young people. "It's not just you," he says. "See, this is the part that was hardest on me, too. I was doing what I was doing and I got arrested. Well, what about my folks? What about your family? They didn't do anything, they're completely innocent. The biggest guilt that I had to deal with was the fact that my parents had to suffer for five years for something I did."

He speaks fast and with confidence that his message is true and important. He's had plenty of time to think this out. "You know, after a while I accepted the fact that I'm in jail. I did it and now I'll go on leading my life. But my folks were outside totally innocent and day after day after day after day they had to deal with me being locked up. And that tore me up."

Billy Hayes says he's not surprised that Americans continued to get into trouble with the law in Turkey, and other dangerous ports of call, well after *Midnight Express* was published and the movie produced. "Even when you're looking at a movie or you're reading a book, it lasts two hours. I mean, movies—it's like rolling over us. We see so many movies, we see so many horror stories, and they roll right by. You're eating popcorn or your ice cream and then you go out and you go home and they smoke a joint and they go off and say, 'Yeah, that was a wild movie!' But the reality of it is that it is not a movie. This is real life. This is happening all over the world." His voice is intense; he sounds almost like an evangelist as he finishes his message with, "Don't let it happen to you."

Hayes realized quickly that the American government was not going to come to his rescue. "They are not a priority, that's the truth" he says about Americans arrested abroad, especially those facing drug charges. "There's very little the government can do," he believes, "even if they wanted to. There's very little they can do to affect the laws of another country. For the United States to intervene on someone's part, they would have to give up some kind of big bargaining chip, and the bottom line is they don't want to for some kid busted with drugs."

Hayes believes it is impossible for an American to be treated in a manner equivalent to the treatment of local citizens. Ensuring that such equal handling exists is the basic goal of the American consul when a U.S. national is arrested overseas. "If the system was the same all over, if the jails were the same and legalities were the same, there wouldn't be such an imbalance. But the fact that you are an American in a foreign prison, you're already at a disadvantage. You don't speak their language, you don't understand their customs, and you will be treated as fairly as possible, but you are going to get the short end of the stick because you can't deal with their legal system. You have all of these legal vultures swooping down upon you trying to take advantage of you and your family, telling people at home that for ten thousand dollars, 'I can get your son free. I know the judge.' Or they make up some ridiculous thing and they'll say, 'We need the money right now, quick because the kid's going to be transferred to a heavy-duty jail and you can't imagine what'll happen to him there.' They're working on the emotions of the family and people are being ripped off; they get tens of thousands of dollars taken away and their son still stays in jail."

Besides giving advice, Billy Hayes is ready to analyze himself and the changes five years in a Turkish prison forced on his personality. "I thought I was invincible. I thought I was immune. I grew up. That's the problem, I think—most people in the United States have such an easy life and they never really have to face some really hard stuff. I mean, we think we do. You don't have a date for the prom or you don't make the football team or your grades. But really that's not real nitty-gritty life-and-death stuff. That's not really being forced into finding out how strong you are or how weak you are. And accepting both of those. It's so wonderful, most people just take it for granted, living in the States. They accept the fact that legally we have all these rights and protections. And it's only when you leave and see how other countries operate and realize that most places in the world do not have the civil rights, the human freedoms that we have here, that you begin to appreciate them. I'm sure there are inequities and people go to jail who shouldn't. But I think it works quite well. It's the best that I've seen, anyway."

Hayes is accustomed now to the role of advisor, especially to young Americans. "It's a big world; you have to go out into it and take your chances," he says knowingly. "That's the bottom line. But you should know what you're doing. Be aware of what's happening. It's not a lark. I mean, there's a lot of pitfalls out there." The contrasts come back to him repeatedly. "It's so safe here. Which is wonderful. That's not a condemnation in any way. It's wonderfully safe here. You can drive across the country and basically feel assured that you're okay and it's thousands of miles. But you can go to Europe or Southeast Asia and thousands of miles includes an incredible array of people, countries, laws, and situations—or lawless situations. Things are different out there in the big world. I think it's good that young Americans get out of the United States and see other countries and realize how fortunate we are."

That's exactly what Gene LePere was doing. If Billy Hayes was the quintessential opportunistic casualty, Gene LePere was the opposite. In her fifties when she traveled to Turkey, she later wrote about her lack of concern as she left on a cruise that included stops in Turkish ports. "Only drug-seeking youngsters encounter trouble with Turkish authorities. We, the hard-working, middle-aged, respectable tourists, feel no identification with these hapless souls. Our attitude has ever been, 'It's their own fault.' Yes, a trip into Turkey still held the illusion of adventure, a hint of danger, the promise of romance – all under the protection of an American passport."

LePere was on a cruise, and the ship put in at a Turkish port. She was approached by a street vendor who pushed three stone masks at her, souvenirs she didn't want. She thought they were poor reproductions of Roman antiquities. But he was insistent; finally she gave him twenty dollars to get rid of him and stuffed what she thought was junk into her shopping bag. When LePere's bags were checked by Turkish customs agents before she reboarded her ocean liner, the masks attracted attention.

She was detained while a Turkish archaeologist was called and identified one of the three masks as a genuine antiquity. As the State Department now cautions American travelers in an official travel advisory, "Unauthorized purchase or removal from Turkey of antiquities or other important cultural artifacts is strictly forbidden. Violation of this law may result in imprisonment. Travelers who wish to purchase such items should always obtain from the seller a receipt and the official museum export certificate required by law."

Not only was LePere unfamiliar with the Turkish law, she had no desire to buy antiquities and did not dream that the twenty dollars' worth of goods foisted on her could have included a national protected treasure. Nonetheless she was taken to Buca Prison, charged with smuggling, and denied bail.

As she waited, expecting help from her government and family, she started to adjust to life in the Buca women's cell, a dormitory filled with a few dozen women. In her book, *Never Pass This Way Again*, she tried to describe her feelings.

|||||||||||||||||||||||| Finally home from her Turkish prison nightmare, New York businesswoman Gene LePere poses with some of the trinkets purchased on her trip. (Photo: Bob Adelman)

Eyes closed, I could hardly imagine a time when I would feel comfortable here. Would I ever recover from this leaden weariness? It robbed me of strength and will. As exposure familiarized me with prison life, I felt increasingly dislocated and disbelieving, encased in a thick fog of unreality that made everything outside myself remote and far away.

What was I doing in this strange world? All that had happened since the dock was a dream, a nightmare I dared to think would vaporize when I awakened. Would I find myself home, on my own familiar bed with the cats purring at my side? Or was home the dream and this the reality?

Lying there, in the eye of the storm, I listened to the unique noises of the hive: the clang of metal against metal where nearby water was being boiled for tea; the brush of clogs against cement as women pursued their limited lives; water gushing from the never-to-be-repaired faucets; and water cascading to the floor and sloshed about with a mop made of torn blankets, spreading the scourge of bone-chilling dampness.

From the squawk box on the wall came unexpected bursts of staccato Turkish rending the air with official announcements and competing with the hollow, rhythmic beating of the palms against the bottom of an overturned plastic pail as women downstairs entertained themselves dancing.

Aside from the horror of incarceration, LePere was never abused in prison and her cellmates catered to her needs. "It's grim," she said of Buca after her release and escape from Turkey. "It's not really evil, but it's grim. It's prison."

After three and a half weeks, the court reversed itself and allowed her release on bail until her trial. "The trauma of events beginning on the dock had damaged some essential aspect of my ego. I was not the same," she described her condition after getting out of prison in her book. "In part, debilitation was responsible. Continuous stress had emptied my reservoirs of energy and courage." Months after she was home in the States, that trauma still plagued her; she still did not feel safe. She told a television interviewer she suffered from post–traumatic stress syndrome. "There is that sense of having been personally violated, having been depersonalized." LePere likened her experience to rape. "There's a shock element. There's no way to explain it; it's not rational."

Friends, lawyers, and American government representatives in Izmir counseled her to stay in Turkey for her trial, trying to convince her that she surely would be acquitted of the charges. Instead she obtained a new passport from the U.S. consulate. Her old passport had been stamped invalid for departure from the country by the Turkish authorities because of her pending trial. The new one was initially insufficient too because it lacked an entry stamp; there was nothing in it to indicate that she had arrived in Turkey legally. She sent it by courier back to her port of entry and obtained a letter stating that the port records documented her arrival. Such a letter is not uncommon, because periodically travelers must replace passports that are lost or stolen.

LePere's escape was possible either because of the inefficiency of the Turkish bureaucracy or because the Turkish government decided to allow her to escape to reduce the international publicity her case was causing. She flew to Ankara and booked a flight on to Germany. Although she had been told her name was on a passport control list, she was stamped out of Turkey with no problem and flew to Munich. "I wanted to get down and kiss the damned floor, to kiss the clean and shining walls," she wrote about her arrival. "Self-consciousness alone prevented it. And the irony of these feelings didn't escape me. To feel such peace, such security and absolute safety in Germany, seemed a cruel joke on a Jew."

Had she followed the advice she was given, LePere's nightmare would have lasted much longer. Her case was tried in absentia. Before the process was completed and she was finally found innocent, there was not just one, but seven trials, conducted over a period of eight months.

Old World Sentences

> Whatever shall we do in that remote spot? Well, we
> will write our memoirs. Work is the scythe of time.
>
> Napoleon Bonaparte, on board HMS *Bellerophon*
> en route to exile in St. Helena in 1815

|||||||||||||||||||| The prison in Draguignan, a delicate French medieval village, is a serious operation. Ultramodern, it is equipped with the latest automatic doors, bulletproof glass, and probing guard towers. It not only looks impossible to escape from, it looks absolutely impregnable to unauthorized visitors.

The U.S. consul in Marseilles discourages me from trying to get into the Draguignan prison, suggesting that the prison director's required approval would be nearly impossible to obtain. I know that there is an intriguing American locked up behind the austere concrete walls: a poet I have been told about by the U.S. consul down the Riviera in Nice, a poet who would undoubtedly wish to talk.

I spend a couple of days enjoying the view of the Mediterranean from my Cannes hotel, working on a plan to get past the guards, and finally decide to try to use the techniques that worked in the Third World. I am armed with the prisoner's name. Leaving my press credentials at the hotel, I show up unannounced at the prison front gate. Using just a few words of French, abundant sign language, and some help from two men who are passing by, I make it clear to the guard at the front gate that I want to get into the prison to see my friend David Eaton.

The guards check my request with Eaton, who – although he has no advance warning and does not know me or about me – says a visit is fine with him. I am told to come back next Saturday during regular visiting hours. It is a Wednesday, a sparkling and sunny day in the south of France, an ideal place to be forced to wait for a few days. But my itinerary calls for me to be far from Draguignan next Saturday. I petition the guards further, trying to explain the importance of my schedule. They check with their superior about this pushy American and finally say, "Okay, come back at visiting time this afternoon."

I kill the time in the warm sun, enjoying the fresh, soft breeze at a sidewalk café, sipping a café au lait while trying to figure out how I might get a tape recorder into the prison with me. When I return to the front gate after lunchtime, I am equipped with a copy of the *International Herald Tribune* and the tiny tape recorder I have been using to record interviews with prisoners. In addition to the recording machine, I carry two commercially recorded music cassettes and a set of earphones. My idea is to tell the guards that the newspaper and the tape player and cassettes are presents for my friend's entertainment. I plan to simply punch the record button, record our interview over one of the music tapes, and then leave the tape recorder with Eaton. The machine is well worth sacrificing for the recorded interview.

The efficient guards find the recorder in my knapsack quickly. It sets off the buzzer when I am forced to pass through two metal detectors as part of the search process. Despite my complaints, the guards confiscate not only the tape machine, but also the newspaper.

Once relieved of my contraband, I am led down sanitized concrete hallways and find myself locked in a tiny visiting room with Eaton. He confirms that he has agreed to visit with me because he is curious. An older, complacent man, Eaton is no stranger to prison. Financial frauds are his game. He is serving his time for passing bad checks, which have already cost him time behind bars in the Netherlands and Germany. "I'm well treated," he tells me, "I've got no complaints. I'm not angry. I'm over twenty-one. If I make an error in judgment, that goes on my account."

He can distinguish no difference in his treatment because he is an American. His French language skills are adequate for his prison needs and he says he is particularly pleased by the attention he receives from the U.S. consul in Marseilles. "I'm surprised visits from the consul take place," he tells me. "I did not know such a service existed." He is particularly pleased that the consul met with the prison director. "That couldn't hurt," he says. "I have nothing but admiration for the consular service."

Happy to talk, glad for the companionship, Eaton describes his routine. "This place is not a prison," he smiles, "it's a hotel." His day starts at seven in the morning with a cup of instant coffee. He enjoys two showers a week and could take more if he played sports. Hot water is available to him in his cell. Cigarettes, candy, and Kleenex are available at the prison store. At eight o'clock the workday starts for prisoners with jobs. Work is a diversion in demand; there are more inmates looking for the pastime than there are jobs available. Those without a job can go to the lounge at half past eight, play cards, and watch television.

Lunch comes just before noon. Eaton calls his two meals each day excellent and describes a recent repast of carrot and onion salad, and beef hearts with noodles, topped off with a banana. The afternoon is again spent working or lounging, and the evening in the cells.

Eaton has a place all to himself, "Thank God. My cell is like an inexpensive YMCA room." The room is equipped with a toilet and bars on the window that Eaton describes as "unobtrusive. My window opens with a view of the mountains. This prison is not a prison," he says again, "it's a one-star hotel, with three-star treatment for me."

David Eaton is a poet. "For me, prison is good for poetry writing. I've always wanted to write, but never had enough time. Three months after I was arrested, I woke up with poetry in my mind and started writing and never stopped." He adopts a contemplative tone and recites for me:

> *You stand at the window*
> *Looking out at the sky above and the cement below*
> *And you sense the blowing winds.*
>
> *The seasons change from one to another.*
> *You know because the leaves change their color.*
> *Time passes by*
> *To be measured by your eye*
> *Measurements those outside do not use.*
>
> *You watch the blowing leaves*
> *And you watch the time*
> *And you sense the blowing winds*
> *Because you cannot open your window and feel*
> *   it on your face.*

There are many more where that came from. When we meet, Eaton has been locked up for three and a half years and he has accumulated a cellful of poems, thirty-five hundred, he estimates. He looks forward to publishing the collection and gladly recites another.

Poet and bad-check artist David Eaton calls his years in prison worth it to him. "I can look at my poems and I have a lot of satisfaction from that," he tells me. "Being in prison does not mean one's creativity stops. For many, it starts in prison." He stops talking, and thinks more about his confinement. "Perhaps I'd feel differently if I had a wife and children waiting for me."

A few weeks after our visit, Eaton writes me a long and thoughtful letter about the plight of his fellow Americans in prisons overseas. He offers jailhouse lawyer advice: be polite with police, make no statements, don't expect problems to be solved in a hurry. "Americans need to be aware," Eaton writes, "that in most countries of the world, the law is denunciatory and is investigative. That means that anyone wanting to cause another a problem needs only to denounce him to the police. By law, the police must then investigate. A judge will then decide if the case has merit. You, in effect, prove your innocence, not they your guilt."

Unfortunately, Eaton is correct. Along with the need to prove innocence, many Americans are shocked at the difficulty, often the impossibility, of arranging bail while waiting for their case to be adjudicated in a foreign court. Bail is specifically referred to in the Eighth Amendment to the U.S. Constitution, which guarantees that "excessive bail shall not be required." This clause has been interpreted by some readers of the Constitution to mean that there is no prohibition against denying bail, only that if bail is offered as an option, it must not be "excessive." But other interpretations insist the Eighth Amendment clearly indicates that bail is a right, that by requiring only a fair amount of security the Founding Fathers created a device to prevent citizens from being punished during the period after an arrest and before a trial. In reality, because of a variety of clarifying state and federal laws, most suspects charged with crimes and awaiting trial in America enjoy the opportunity – if they have access to adequate property to satisfy the court – to be released on bail. There are exceptions; courts do at times deny bail when they are convinced that a suspect is a threat to the community or is likely to jump bail. But bail is usually an option after an arrest in America.

The initial shock following arrest in a foreign country – discovering that bail is unlikely or impossible – is numbingly compounded by the next lesson many Americans learn for the first time only after they are arrested overseas. The principle of American law that presumes a citizen is innocent of a crime unless and until proven guilty beyond a reasonable doubt is a judicial philosophy not shared by most of the rest of the world. Although it is not specifically written into the U.S. Constitution, the presumption of innocence, inherited by the colonies from England, was described in detail and specifically reaffirmed in 1895 by the U.S. Supreme Court in the case of *Coffin v. United States*.* The majority ruled in that Indiana bank fraud case that "the principle that there is a presumption of innocence in favor of the accused is the undoubted law, axiomatic and elementary, and its enforcement lies at the foundation of our criminal law." In explaining its position, the Court traced the presumption of innocence back to the Bible on through Roman law and English common law to America.† Justice Edward White joined the Court just before the decision, and his interpretation sums up the attitude most Americans carry as a birthright. "The presumption of innocence," he wrote, "is a conclusion drawn by the law in favor of the citizen, by virtue whereof, when brought to trial upon a criminal charge, he must be acquitted, unless he is proven to be guilty." Too many Americans never learn, or forget, that the rules often change when they leave home.

Many travel destinations for Americans are influenced by the Napoleonic Code, the laws drafted for France by Napoleon in 1804. These statutes spread to conquered territories and were instrumental in the development of laws in much of the rest of the world. The direct result is that Americans detained in most foreign police jurisdictions are presumed guilty until innocence is proven.

Where the most barbaric governments are in control of the judicial process, Americans can find themselves not only presumed guilty, but without a reasonable legal avenue available to try to prove their innocence.

From his one-star French prison, David Eaton writes more details about his satisfaction not only with American consular officers working in

---

* The Supreme Court ruled March 4, 1895, in *Coffin v. United States*, case number 741.

† "Roman law," instructed the Court in its ruling, "was pervaded with the results of this maxim of criminal administration," and it cites several specific mentions of the concept from Roman codes. "Exactly when," explained the Court, "this presumption [of innocence] was, in precise words, stated to be a part of the common law, is involved in doubt." But the court quoted the English jurists Lord Matthew Hale, "It is better five guilty persons should escape unpunished than one innocent person should die," and Sir William Blackstone, "The law holds that it is better that ten guilty persons escape than that one innocent suffer," to buttress the decision.

France, but also with those he encountered while he was serving time in Germany. They provided him with a handbook detailing German law that explained his rights as both a defendant and later as a convicted criminal. It included a glossary of German legal terms. He was provided with English-language books and magazines. "I could not speak highly enough," he writes, "of the support given by the Munich consulate."

Unlike so many other Americans arrested and their friends and relatives, Eaton continues his praise for the American foreign service. "Generally speaking, the consulates are not responsible that we are in trouble. That the U.S. government took this much interest in what happens to its less praiseworthy citizens sitting in foreign prisons came as a surprise to me. I'm sure the consulates get more blame than praise, but it should be the reverse. Their people work hard, and are not overpaid, for being there."

Perhaps because he was found guilty of a crime, acknowledges that guilt, and is held in such civilized accommodations, his attitude toward consulate services differs radically from that of many other Americans facing foreign police, courts, and prisons. Enclosed with his letter are more poems.

After Mexico and Canada, the greatest number of Americans imprisoned overseas are in Germany. Besides the tourists who pass through this country, unified Germany is still home base to thousands of U.S. troops. Many soldiers who serve tours of duty in Germany decide to stay there. The mere presence of so many Americans within Germany's borders partially explains the large population of Americans in German prisons.

There is a double standard for Americans locked up in Germany. Civilians are at the mercy of the German courts. For soldiers, it's different. They are subject to an agreement made in the aftermath of World War II and still in effect between the German and American governments. Called the Status of Forces Agreement, it gives the U.S. military jurisdiction when crimes are perpetrated by U.S. soldiers on German territory. Similar agreements keep Americans out of the local courts in some other countries, like Korea, where a large number of U.S. troops are permanently stationed.

Through a lawyer who represents Americans in Germany, I arrange to interview a former GI sentenced to the maximum security prison in Frankfurt, a prison filled with violent criminals and political activists incarcerated by the German government for terrorism. The prison is a combination of old and modern buildings incongruously situated in a quiet residential neighborhood. The institution's walls are high slabs of concrete, topped with rolls of fierce-looking concertina wire.

At the main gate, I turn in my passport and pass through a set of two automatic steel doors. First the outside door opens, allowing me into a limbo space where I wait while that first door is closed and locked. Then the next door opens, giving me access to the main office of the complex. The security technology is superior, a far cry from the circus atmosphere at Karachi City Prison, with the one guard at the old iron gate collecting his bribes.

The next stop is an X-ray machine. I put my bag in to be checked. Inside is my large tape recorder. On top of the bag, I set down my tiny tape recorder, the one that the French authorities had not permitted into the Draguignan prison. The television monitor displays the wires and other electronic components of the equipment.

"What's this?" asks the guard operating the machine. I tell him it is a tape recorder, and he consults with a colleague. While they mull over the regulations regarding recording equipment, I slip the tiny machine back into my pocket. Then I dig the large machine out of my bag and push it at the guards. I tell them I don't really need the machine that they have discovered and ask them to keep it while I visit the prisoner. They take it and check it into a locker, and I go off to record my interview. Smuggling the tape machine into the Frankfurt prison is an inconsequential victory, and undoubtedly not worth the risk. But for some silly reason it gives me a sense of satisfaction. After witnessing some of the most miserable and bizarre prisons in the world, it is actually fun to violate the efficient German security, even for such an insignificant goal.

The prisoner is called and I face another hurdle. He hasn't been told in advance of my visit. He doesn't know who I am nor why I am there to see him. In the corridor outside the visiting room, there are a few moments of tension as he looks at me in confusion and asks the guards about me. So I start talking with him, speaking fast, explaining my mission, working hard to convince him to sit still for an interview. The guards look irritated and keep interrupting, asking him if he wants to talk with me. Finally, he agrees and we are ushered into a room alone. There is nothing inside but a table and two chairs. The solid door is fitted with a peephole. I take the tape recorder out of my pocket, point it at the prisoner, and shroud it with my back. I listen to his tale until the guard bangs on the door, announcing the end of the visit.

Breakfast is served at seven: bread with marmalade, coffee, sometimes with an egg, sometimes with wurst or cheese. Then he goes to work in the library, "It's better than sitting in the cell," until lunchtime. Again the food sounds quite civilized after hearing about so much Third World gruel. Lunch is potatoes, meat, and salad or fruit. Then it's back to the library until a light dinner. After four the cell door is locked until the next morning.

He lives alone. "It's small. My cell is okay. There are other cells where the walls are dirty and there's writing like, 'American go home,' and stuff like this. But in my cell, it's been recently cleaned and painted. It's nice." He has a private toilet and sink. His room comes with a radio that receives not only German broadcasts, but also the American Armed Forces Network station.

He tells me he has been in prison just over a year. "I hurt somebody," is his initial explanation. He had been a soldier, stationed in Germany for a year and a half. After his tour of duty, he stayed because he liked Germany. Like so many convicts, he starts his story with a disclaimer. "My case is not like the average case." Then he realizes how hackneyed he sounds. "Everybody says that, but my case is not the same. The best way I can put it is that I let external influences take control of my own life. I wasn't in control of my own life. It doesn't matter if it was alcohol or drugs, it got the better of me, so now I have to take the consequences." He was sentenced to three and a half years for a senseless knife attack on a woman he did not know whom he ran into by chance on a Frankfurt street. She was slightly injured and he was arrested for assault and battery, tried, and convicted.

But neither his nationality nor his crime seems to make his stay in prison difficult. "I've met a couple terrorists that were here because of bombings of American military. I mean they were actually in charge of putting the bombs in the car. And I got along with them okay. Why? Because they knew I wasn't military. I was a civilian." He says he finds no national prejudice inside the prison. "Everybody is totally the same here. There is no land that is better than another. Here we're all prisoners and the feeling is mutual."

It is his first time in prison, his first time arrested, he says. "As far as prison life, staying in, I can handle it personally. But when you have something outside, like a family, it tears them up." His son was born after he was caught. "Every day I hear someone new saying that their family has left or the wife's gone out with another guy or that the children are having a hard time. It's just terrible."

Like David Eaton, this Frankfurt prisoner is a fan of the U.S. consul. "They're fantastic, I have to say that. They send books twice a month. They come to visit once a month. It's short, but they're doing it. They say, 'Ah, you're still alive. Are they still feeding you?' For me, they've helped me a lot personally. They've given me all the paperwork for the visa for my girlfriend. They'll do what you need if they can do it. If they can't, then they'll tell you they can't."

Despite the mindless and heinous crime he committed, he comes up with some sobering reflections. "At the same time that I realize the responsibility I have to pay society for what I did, I realize that this is bad because there is only one life to live." He compares himself with the career criminals in his midst and says, "Oh my gosh, I don't belong here. I did something wrong. But there were better solutions. I could have gone into treatment, the possibilities were there." Then he worries for his future because of the jailhouse education he's receiving. "What I fear is that when I get out I'll know more about how things are not supposed to be done. Like people have told me the A through Z on how to get a false passport when I get back to the States. I don't want to know that. I don't want to be even tempted to do that. I always kept away from that. But I know it now, it doesn't matter if I want to or not. You can't close yourself in, even if you're in a cell by yourself. You have that contact to murderers, to people from these countries that live like pigs. In this way I feel that prison is not right."

He wants to get through his sentence without word getting home that he has been sent to jail. He doesn't want his mother to know what happened. "I do have pride in being my mom's son. She knows that I did things in my life, but not so, so drastic. Even when I can't answer to myself why I did this, then it's going to be fifty times harder to answer it to my mom. And that I've tried to avoid."

The guard knocks.

One of the more famous Americans to wind up behind the bars of a foreign prison was the actor Stacey Keach, arrested for carrying cocaine into London's Heathrow Airport and charged with smuggling.

During his trial, Keach admitted regularly using the drug, "as a means of trying to alleviate exhaustion, trying to maintain one's concentration." He then renounced the drug and its use saying, "One of the diabolical things about cocaine is that it gives you a false sense of security and gives you a momentary sense of energy which is immediately followed by depression. I can't deny the deep humiliation and embarrassment for what's happened. I am terribly sorry for what has happened, not that I was caught but that I have caused my family and business colleagues a tremendous sense of anything but pride. I can only hope that I can make amends by, as a public person, taking a public posture in trying to help other people in rehabilitation." Despite the speech, Keach was convicted, sentenced to nine months, and taken off to jail.

Keach served his time at a lonesome old stone prison in Reading, England. There he was a trustie, librarian, and fodder for endless tabloid copy. "Stacey Keach," proclaimed the *National Enquirer,* "TV's tough-as-nails Mike Hammer, turned into a quivering wreck after only days in a tough English prison." The *Enquirer* insisted that Keach was a target of threats from other convicts who wanted to fight him both because he was an American and because he played a detective on television.

A few weeks after Keach was locked up, two of his friends arrived at Reading, and fueled rumors that Keach was being mistreated after they were refused the opportunity to visit with him. One of the friends was playwright and actor Jason Miller, who left the prison telling reporters he was worried about Keach's health and safety. The British Home Office, which supervises all British prisons, responded to the worries and the tabloid reports with the statement, "He is not ill. He hasn't been assaulted. He hasn't been in any fight. The story that's circulating is a figment of somebody's imagination." When asked why Keach's friends were turned away from Reading, the Home Office answered correctly, "You can't simply knock at the door of a British prison and expect to see somebody. Visits are regulated. They are rationed. They take time to arrange and are allowed only when the prisoner wishes the visit and the governor approves." At the time, Keach was allowed only one visit a month.

But Keach's friends were right to worry. Foreign prisons can be dangerous—life threatening—for Americans. At the beginning of 1990, an American charged with drug trafficking and waiting for a trial was attacked by five other inmates in his cell at El Pavon Penitentiary in Guatemala. Gordon Krekow, Jr., died a few hours after the stabbing, which was apparently motivated by robbery.

After six months in Reading, the actor was released. He said the prison staff treated him "with respect and compassion and without special privileges." He went back to Heathrow and before boarding a Concorde to New York said with a smile, "I feel terrific! Freedom is the best feeling in the world. Prison taught me a lot of things. It teaches you a lot of humility." It was a typically chilly and gray London day. "In spite of the weather," said Keach, "it's one of the happiest moments of my life. It feels great to be free, and thank God that I'm alive and standing on this side of the wall."

Although there were suggestions at the time that Keach received a short sentence because of his celebrity status, his case shows that, like the U.S. government, fame and money cannot necessarily keep an American out of jail overseas.

Beating the Lagos
Firing Squad

> Those who have gotten out have always told me
> that the one thing that gave them hope and the one
> thing they think ultimately won their release was
> the fact that their case wasn't allowed to become ob-
> scure, that it was kept on the front pages, and that
> in the end – for one reason or another – the [foreign]
> government decided that it was wiser to let them go
> than to try to detain them.
>
> > New York Congressman William Green
> > at a 1985 meeting publicizing the plight
> > of Marie McBroom

||||||||||||||||||| **O**nce in a unfortunate while, professional evaluation of
the conditions for Americans at foreign prisons from an insider's point
of view is made possible because a reporter is arrested.

In the summer of 1980, still another military government took control of Bolivia when General Luis García Meza led a bloody military
coup. The general's henchmen knew that fair news reports were dangerous for the new government and targeted the international press corps.
American journalist Mary Ellen Spooner, a correspondent for several
American, Canadian, and British publications, was among those arrested. After being locked up and terrorized for six days, she was
deported and filed a dispatch about her ordeal.

She was arrested at her hotel by plainclothes officers she identified as
being from the Interior Ministry. That first day she was "interrogated,
harassed and threatened by officials, including the interior minister himself, Col. Luis Arce Gomez, who had apparently ordered my arrest."

Spooner reported that on her first day in custody, she was accused of writing lies about Bolivia and the chief interrogator asked her how she wanted to die. "Gesturing toward the window," Spooner wrote in the Canadian news magazine *Maclean's*, "he asked how I'd like to be tossed several storeys to the ground. Pointing to a pistol he carried in a shoulder holster, he asked if I preferred bullets. Had I ever visited a plastic surgeon? Because I was going to need one now, he threatened." Another interrogator warned her that if she did not answer questions with the responses the new government wanted to hear, "they are going to use force and as a woman there are certain things that can happen to you." At one point, she reported, Arce Gomez raged at Spooner, "We're going to cut off your head."

She spent six days locked in a closet, allowed out only to use the toilet. Meals were black coffee, rice, potatoes, and meat. She was not allowed to bathe or change her clothes.

The general's Bolivian Information Ministry told the world Spooner was arrested for "spreading lies" about Bolivia. Among the new government's complaints was a story she filed for the *Economist* detailing alleged government involvement in cocaine traffic from Bolivia. Facing charges that carried as much as fifteen years in prison, Spooner was finally deported after her editors from the *Economist* and the *Financial Times* flew to La Paz from London to lobby for her release. She left Bolivia calling it South America's Uganda.

Late in 1986, Associated Press correspondent John Edlin was apprehended on the streets of Lusaka, Zambia. He was jailed without being charged for five days before being flown back home to his base in Zimbabwe. He credited lobbying by Western diplomats for his release, and once safe out of Zambia filed a frightening account describing life in Kamwala Remand Prison.

"In a colonial-era prison built for 80," wrote Edlin in an AP dispatch, "more than 500 men and boys, some as young as seven years old, exist day-to-day amid filth and vermin, under constant threat of beatings, deprived of meat, medicine and almost all hope."

Eldin determined that some of his fellow inmates had been locked up without being charged for as many as four years. He landed in Kamwala after being declared a "prohibited immigrant." He assumed his detention was connected to news stories he wrote about anti-government food riots that followed food price increases in Zambia.

"For those five nights," wrote Edlin, "I shared Cellblock 3 – a mere

15 paces by 9 paces—with 108 other inmates, sleeping on lice-ridden gray blankets spread over the concrete floor."

Although Edlin did not report any abuse directed against him, his dispatch described a monstrous institution. "Some of the twenty or so juveniles in the prison were routinely sodomized by trusties—convicts designated as cell captains—after lights out at 9 P.M. One twelve-year-old named Phiri told me he was given cigarettes for such favors. The captains punished prisoners by punching them on the small of the back repeatedly with clenched fists. One inmate, bound hand and foot, was beaten eighteen times in one night by the trusties. Prisoners also were punished for failure to keep Cellblock 3's single pit latrine clean, for speaking disrespectfully to the captains, and for being late in line for the two daily meals—of corn-meal porridge, peanuts and boiled beans infested with live cockroaches. Beef was delivered each day, but the deliveries were commandeered by trusties and given to prison officials in return for cigarettes, marijuana and matches."

Edlin determined that most of the convicts in Kamwala were unemployed petty criminals. Some of those not convicted of any crime, but locked up for indeterminate amounts of time, told him they did not know why they had been incarcerated.

Reporter Edlin characterized his treatment by the prison's superintendent Stanford Tembo as "sympathetic." When Edlin finally was released, he says Tembo told him, "I'm glad you're going. You shouldn't have been here in the first place. Nor should half of these people."

Marie McBroom was not as lucky as John Edlin. The New Jersey businesswoman spent a year in a miserable Nigerian prison retroactively charged with a commercial crime, a crime that the Nigerian government threatened to punish with execution. This horror story began routinely, as so many do.

Marie McBroom was no stranger to Africa. She traveled there often, doing business as a trader. She bought African goods for export, such as cement, rice, and other foods. As a black American, she often expressed an affinity for Africa and a desire to engage in fair business exchanges that would ultimately benefit Africans.

In the summer of 1983, the fifty-seven-year-old grandmother made another excursion to Nigeria, this time seeking new export contracts. While she was still working out her arrangements in Lagos, the military overthrew the civilian government and tossed McBroom into prison.

She wasn't the only victim of the coup. Amnesty International estimates that 475 businesspeople and politicians were arrested by the new government on a variety of charges. The arrests were called part of a "war against indiscipline," supposedly carried out to rid the country of corruption. New laws were enacted making food smuggling, counterfeiting, and unauthorized oil trafficking capital crimes.

Marie McBroom had been negotiating oil export contracts, but for months she was held without being charged with any crime. Initially, she just disappeared without a trace from her room in the Lagos Holiday Inn. When her two daughters, Dana Manno and Marcia McBroom Landess, routinely tried to reach her at the Holiday Inn from their homes in New York City, they were told she had checked out and left no new address.

In violation of international agreements, the Nigerian government did not notify the U.S. embassy in Lagos of the arrest for two months. Consequently, whenever the sisters asked embassy officials to check on their mother's whereabouts, their concerns were dismissed. The embassy insisted that McBroom could not have been arrested because if she had been, the Nigerians would honor their commitments and inform the Americans.

When an American businessman who knew McBroom in Lagos told the sisters that he believed McBroom had been arrested, they stepped up their pressure on the embassy staff to look into her disappearance. Finally the Nigerians acknowledged holding McBroom.

It wasn't until more than nine months after her arrest that McBroom faced charges. She was first accused of illegal currency trading, charges that were then dismissed and replaced with accusations of illegal petroleum trafficking. In a bizarre decree issued by the military government five months after McBroom was arrested, transactions such as those McBroom had been conducting before the decree went into effect and before the military government was in power became illegal. The specific charge was exporting petroleum products without a proper permit. Death by firing squad was the penalty.

As bleak as the outlook for their mother was, the sisters soon learned that McBroom's day-to-day life was grim, also. They were contacted by another American businesswoman who had been held for forty days with McBroom. Dorothy Davies told the sisters that the two of them lived with up to five other women in a ten-foot-square room. They slept on the floor, alongside the dirty hole that was their toilet. For a pad they shared a rug fouled with old urine. There were no blankets or sheets, no change of clothes or bathing facilities. The heat was oppressive, the food unacceptable.

Davies managed to convince her jailers to release her, saying she needed to visit her sick mother back in the United States. Presumably it was an unauthorized release, because the State Department later said its sources in Nigeria reported the guards who let her go were jailed themselves. Marie McBroom was moved to Kiri-Kiri Prison, a maximum security facility in Lagos.

As Nigeria finally prepared to try McBroom on the oil trading charges, her daughters staged a support rally at the Community Church in New York. There they talked about their limited involvement in their mother's case.

"We hear very little, that's been one of our hopes, even to just get a card or letter from my mother so we can have some sort of direct contact with her," complained Dana Manno. "The only contact we have is through the American embassy. Things are just very grave," she said. "We don't know what will happen next. We're waiting for the decision from the tribunal." The frustration and anxiety of feeling helpless in the face of tragedy was apparent in her voice. "Everyone that has been brought in front of the tribunal has been sentenced to death. So we don't know, regardless of what evidence they are given, what the outcome will be."

Manno's sister, Marcia Landess, expressed pessimism about her mother's future because Nigerian government officials were publicly insisting McBroom was guilty. Such statements, said Landess, made her "tremble."*

Landess worried about the severe conditions she was told her mother was facing in Kiri-Kiri. "It's very hard to survive in a foreign jail for people with our standard of living in America," she said at the rally. "You could imagine not being able to bathe for forty days in sweltering heat, being fed irregularly, having everything one eats filled with pepper, having to sleep on a concrete floor." Landess speculated that not knowing her fate from one day to the next was one of the worst hardships facing her mother.

---

*Landess not only knew Africa, Africa knew her. Under the name Susie Martins, she had been the model used by Lever Brothers to sell Lux soap throughout the continent. Her likeness was also used by UNICEF to advocate breast-feeding instead of commercial formulas for infants.

The sisters appealed to the Nigerian government to recognize all the positive work their mother had contributed over the years to African development and let McBroom go free. "It reminds me," said Manno, "of Joseph in the Bible, when he was incarcerated due to false testimony. But it ended up he was exonerated by the very people who captured him. I could hope something like that happens in the end."

McBroom's daughters brought Theodore Simon and the International Legal Defense Counsel into the case, hoping that their experience could help. The ILDC lawyers enjoy a deserved reputation for understanding many of the problems facing Americans arrested overseas, and devising productive plans of action for prisoners and their friends and families. From Billy Hayes to Marie McBroom, their client list includes many of the more notorious cases of Americans in foreign prisons.

The ILDC has carved out a niche as a leading source for dealing with the crisis of overseas legal and human rights questions for Americans. One of the firm's rallying points is the adoption of prisoner transfer treaties. The U.S. government has negotiated and ratified such treaties with a wide variety of foreign governments, but not all the countries where Americans are imprisoned are signatories to such treaties. There are agreements in effect with Mexico and Canada, the two countries where historically the greatest numbers of Americans come in conflict with the local law. A treaty is in effect with most of the Western European countries under the umbrella of the Council of Europe, with Panama, Peru, Bolivia, Thailand, and that most infamous of foreign jurisdictions for Americans worried about serving time overseas, Turkey.

Transfer treaties do not mean that the problems Americans face in foreign jails disappear. The opportunity to transfer is available only after a prisoner passes through the police and court systems of a foreign judicial system and is convicted and sentenced. Often the worst abuse that a prisoner faces is during the period of arrest, interrogation, and investigation of an alleged crime. The treaties require that all trial proceedings be completed; therefore, a certain portion of a prisoner's sentence is always served in the country where the crime supposedly took place. Once back in the United States, a transferred prisoner is eligible for parole or conditional release. The determination of whether or not to grant such release is based on a study of the crime in relation to U.S. law. Any credit for good time or labor that the prisoner earned overseas is applicable to the parole request.

But unlike prisoners who serve out their sentences in foreign jurisdictions, a transferred prisoner is burdened with a record in America of criminal behavior overseas. Not that completing a sentence overseas guarantees that there will be no notation of the conviction back at home. In 1982 President Reagan ordered the CIA, the FBI, the Drug Enforcement Agency, and a host of other government agencies to start seeking information internationally about Americans involved in drug trafficking. ILDC lawyer Simon says that it is common – especially in countries like Mexico and Peru where the DEA maintains a high profile – for the DEA to know about the arrest of an American well before U.S. consular officials are notified by the Peruvian or Mexican authorities. In addition, the U.S. government maintains arrangements with Germany and Turkey, two countries where many Americans are imprisoned, to routinely exchange information on the criminal convictions of each other's citizens.

Transfer treaties require that the prisoner seeking to go home to America be serving time in the foreign prison for a crime that is also a crime in America. No transfer can occur without the consent of all three parties in the affair: the country where the prisoner is locked up, the United States, and the prisoner. Most transfer requests from Americans are approved by foreign governments.

The treaty with Thailand requires that prisoners serve as many as eight years in Thailand before they can be eligible for transfer back to the United States. Negotiation of the treaty was difficult. Thailand wanted to ensure that its judicial sovereignty was not infringed upon, and some American government representatives were worried about appearing to be soft toward drug traffickers. Most of the Americans imprisoned in Thailand are held for drug offenses.

During the debate over the treaty in 1984, Florida Senator Paula Hawkins was involved because of her membership on the Senate Foreign Relations Committee. She didn't just want heroin dealers locked up. "It's bewildering to foreign countries," she said at the time about American attitudes toward traffickers. "They say to me, 'We have the death penalty, why don't you have the death penalty?' I say, 'Because I don't have the votes.' I'd go for the death penalty myself. I think [trafficking] is dealing in mass murder."

The final treaty includes another clause unique to the Thai agreement. Inmates convicted of transporting more than one kilogram of heroin are considered "inappropriate" for transfer by the terms of the

treaty and can be considered for a transfer only under "extraordinary circumstances," such as providing law enforcement authorities with information leading to the arrest and conviction of other traffickers.

As a strong advocate of prisoner transfer treaties, lawyer Theodore
Simon is particularly sensitive to the disregard expressed for the welfare
of Americans locked up on drug charges by former Senator Hawkins and
the American consular officer I spoke with in Bangkok, Fred Vogel.
"The United States has been pursuing a strong international law enforcement policy aimed especially at illicit drug smuggling," he wrote
in the *Pacific Law Journal*. "Regardless of the wisdom of that policy, the
policy is certainly not in conflict with a fundamental concern for the welfare of United States citizens abroad. For decades, the correctional
policy of the United States has been aimed at a rehabilitative, as well as
punitive, approach toward a prisoner. This method has included the
promotion of the social reintegration of the offender into society in
general and the offender's family in particular, as exemplified by the use
of halfway houses. The use of prisoner transfer treaties can be seen as
a logical extension of this philosophy."

With less legal foundation, but more poignantly, Simon makes this
argument in favor of transferring Americans out of foreign misery: "Protecting the inherent dignity of a human being is not contradictory to a
policy of strict law enforcement."*

Since the transfer treaties were first ratified in the mid-seventies,
hundreds of Americans have become eligible to use them and subse-
quently return, as did Chris Rincon, to the relative safety of an American prison and then parole.

The details of international transfer treaties were a moot point to Marie
McBroom as she awaited her trial in Kiri-Kiri prison in Lagos. There
is no transfer treaty between the United States and Nigeria.

Suffering from malaria, glaucoma, and a broken toe, forty-five pounds
underweight and with hair turned to gray, she finally was brought before
the military tribunal that charged her with the retroactive wrongdoing.

---

*The entire text of Simon's article surveying U.S. transfer treaties, written with
Robert Pisani, who was then executive director of the ILDC, can be found in the *Pacific
Law Journal*, spring 1986, volume 17. Another article by Simon and law partner
Richard Atkins offers advice on how to best take advantage of the treaties. Titled *Crea-
tive and Effective Use of Prisoner Transfer Treaties*, it is available from ILDC at the
Philadelphia address listed in the bibliography.

The charge was described as "speaking to unknown persons" for the purpose of selling petroleum products or other minerals without a permit from the government.

McBroom pleaded innocent of any crime. She told the court that her intention had been to introduce foreign oil buyers to the Nigerian National Petroleum Corporation. She insisted that her business was legitimate. The prosecution countered with the claim that McBroom conspired with three Nigerians to illegally generate oil sales. The judge ruled that the charges were "not proven beyond reasonable doubt." As quickly as she was arrested a year before at her Holiday Inn room, McBroom was acquitted on all counts. A day later Marie McBroom climbed off an airplane in New York with the words, "Thank God I'm an American! God bless America!"

After a few days' rest, McBroom met with reporters. She expressed appreciation for the work her daughters had done to publicize her case, saying, "If it wasn't for outside pressure, I might still be there." She described the beatings she witnessed in Kiri-Kiri, the terror of listening to the prison firing squads executing other prisoners. "I was more worried about my family than myself, because I knew it was a nightmare for them."

McBroom tried to express the trauma of isolation. "They don't allow you to communicate with anyone," she said of her suffering. "You can't read any newspapers, you can't see anyone. God bless America," she repeated. "I have never been so proud to be an American in my life!"

First World Country Clubs

The prime purpose of any prison system is to carry
out the sanctions imposed by society on members
who have transgressed its rules. And that is what
Canada's correctional system does—but it does so
in a humane way which provides maximum opportunities to those inmates who wish to take advantage of them.

> From *Beyond the Walls*, a booklet published
> by the Correctional Service of Canada

Be a man,
Not a fool.
Do your lag,
And be cool.

> Doggerel carved into a holding cell table
> at Auckland Central Police Station

|||||||||||||||||||| **A**merican Michael St. Germain is describing his daily
routine at the modern and comfortable Paremoremo Prison in Auck-
land, New Zealand. "In the mornings we're unlocked at seven o'clock
and you have a couple of minutes to wash your face and get downstairs
to the dining room where breakfast will be served." Just the terminology
is shocking after listening to the stories of misery in Asia, Africa, and
Latin America: "dining room" and "breakfast will be served" sound in-
congruous in a prison context.

Breakfast is just porridge, explains St. Germain. "You're lucky if you
get eggs and bacon probably twice a week; the rest of the time it's a mix
of either spaghetti or some sort of chops or sometimes sausages, potatoes. It's not too bad." No mention of maggots in the meat. No worry

about disease from rotten food, dysentery from bad water, fights over portions.

After breakfast St. Germain and his colleagues make their beds and head off for their work, which starts at eight o'clock. Woodworking is available; so is laundry and farm work. They take a lunch break for an hour and then go back to the job until dinnertime. After dinner, "We get to go to the gymnasium, which has a real good weight-training room, we have a badminton court, we have indoor soccer, we have volleyball. All different nights of the week we play these different sports. We have lots of sporting activity like that. I get plenty of time to wear myself out physically." St. Germain says once the work and exercise exhaust him, he sleeps well. He's sure his prison time is good for his health, that he'll leave New Zealand in better shape than he came.

His cell is tiny but private, equipped with a bed and a desk. There's a small bookshelf and a toilet and sink. Every night he turns in his clothes to the laundry crew. They are washed and returned to him the next morning clean and dry.

"I was pretty lucky to be an American," St. Germain says of his arrival in the New Zealand prison system. The other inmates were curious about the United States and didn't bother him, just asked him questions about his homeland. "Being an American gave me a chance to be questioned rather than hassled."

The prison gangs, with unnerving names like the Headhunters, left him alone, too, limiting their few fights to tussles with each other. "I did get approached a few times. A big fellow wanted my watch and I just told him to take it and to stick it and if he wants to get the watch he's going to have to take it from me. After hearing my accent, I guess he changed his mind. He goes, 'Oh, an American! You're from America!' And he started talking to me about America. So it got me off the hook and it felt really good."

The New Zealand prisoners wanted to hear stories about American girls, guns, and motorcycles – particularly Harley-Davidsons, since their country mainly imports Triumphs. As a surfer, St. Germain was more familiar with waves and beaches, but he managed to come up with enough Harley stories to keep his fellow prisoners entertained. As for the guards, the worst abuse he reports was when they called him "bloody Yank."

St. Germain came to New Zealand planning on a two-week trip, not a two-year "lag," as the Kiwis call jail time. "I left my girlfriend that I'd been living with for five years and my dog, my house, my boat, and my truck." His girlfriend sold his belongings to pay his fine and court costs. "She's an excellent lady." Suffering the material losses was difficult for him at first, "but you learn to accept it, you've got to, otherwise you're just going to be walking around in a shell. You've got to be able to adjust to it and say, 'Okay, I did that and when I get out, I'll take care of it. I'll be free, I'll be somebody new, and I'll put this behind me, chalk one up for experience.' Like at first I was really broken, you know? I couldn't really handle it. I was saying, 'Oh, my boat's going to go. I lost this nice house, and oh my missus, I'm not going to see her for a long time, until she can get down here.' As it turns out it was seven months before she did make it down here."

St. Germain is in Paremoremo for violating New Zealand's drug laws. With his stories of a private room, bacon and eggs, and laundry service–especially after seeing his compatriots suffering in places like Karachi City Prison and Klong Prem–it's difficult to develop much sympathy for his plight.

The same is the case for prisoners in Canada. "Inmates who've done time in the States look at our system as a piece of cake," says Collins Bay warden Ken Payne from his office in the Kingston, Ontario, penitentiary. He cites smaller prisons, fewer inmates, and the opportunity to get a decent education behind bars as reasons so many Americans decide to serve their time in Canada rather than transfer home.

"There seems to be a perception," he says, "that if you've got to do time, it's better to do it here than in the United States." One reason, he speculates, is that there is less ethnic diversity in Canada and consequently fewer gang problems in prisons. But beyond the racial and cultural issue, he points with pride to the amount of money Canada spends on each prisoner, with the goals of not just punishing, but also providing techniques to "help them do good time, keep them from coming back, and put them back on the street in better shape than they were coming in."

Collins Bay lies just off Lake Ontario in Kingston. It looks forbidding with its guard towers and fences, high walls topped with concertina wire. But most inmates with experience in American prisons are glad to be north of the border.

One of the convicts I talk with was caught with two hundred pounds of marijuana. He says he never thought about the fact that he'd end up

|||||||||||||||||||||||| The severe appearance of Collins Bay belies its country club reputation among most of the American inmates. (Photo: Correctional Service of Canada, Communications Branch)

in a Canadian prison if he were arrested. "I didn't think about it in those terms because I felt that the Canadian system was on a parity with the American system. I found out the hard way that it certainly is not." Not that he's discriminated against in the prison. "As far as the men are concerned," he says, "there is no differentiation other than calling me Yank." He's lived in New York City, Florida, and on the West Coast. "I get many, many questions every day: What's it like? How is it? Is it all it's said it is? Is it all it's cracked up to be? It puts me on some sort of a pedestal. Other than that there is no differentiation."

An older man with bifocals, he smokes Camels as we talk. He is wearing a thermal shirt and running shoes. As much as he enjoys telling the stories about American cities, he's bitter about his experience in the Canadian courts. "I have somewhat coined a term up here. When they use the term *justice*, it means *just us*, meaning the cards are stacked well against the individual here in Canada, unfortunately. It's a far cry from what we have at home. When a policeman says, 'That man did it,' the only way you're not going to jail is if you have irrefutable proof that you did not."

Despite the relatively civilized conditions of Collins Bay, even compared with American prisons like the Atlanta Federal Penitentiary or San Quentin, let alone Third World prisons, he finds plenty to complain about. "Humane in what respect?" he questions. "Until a few short weeks ago we were double-bunked here in one of the blocks. Now I don't know if you've spent any time in a reasonable-sized bathroom, but to have two men in a thirteen- by five-foot cell with no privacy to speak of for twenty-four hours a day, seven days a week, if you want to qualify that as humane, you're entitled to. I certainly do not." Certainly my own perspective is jaded at this point by images like that of Marie McBroom sleeping on the concrete floor in Kiri-Kiri next to the festering cesspool.

He insists that the placid facade presented by the Canadian prison system is deceptive. "Contrary to most thought, it's a life of survival on a day-to-day basis. I'm sure the gentleman over here," he gestures to the guard who is sitting in on the interview as part of the terms of my visit, "would be not willing to reveal statistics, but violence is a part of prison life."

In fact, that guard's superior, warden Payne, is quite forthcoming about the problems of prison violence in Collins Bay. "We've had the worst year, last year, that we've had in the history of this place," he tells me as we discuss the differences between American and Canadian prisons. "We had three murders in a four-month period." Payne complains that, too often, society forgets about problems inherent to a prison population. "Something that is very difficult to get people on the outside to accept is that you're not dealing with a large group of rational people. That's not to say they're all irrational, but they don't resolve their problems the same way most people do." Then he gives an illustration of what he means. "If you and I get in a fight, we'll discuss it," he explains. "Maybe in a bar. I'll say, 'I dislike your beard,' and you say, 'Well, yours is too gray.' And I'll say, 'Well, tough shit.' Somebody else," now he is referring to the inmates in his charge, "will rip your face off." He laughs.

It is no laughing matter for the marijuana smuggler. "Prison violence," he says, "all stems back to the fact that you have many people in here who have been here too long, on baseless charges, on trumped-up charges, sentences which far exceed the crime, if you will. And because of this, there is a tremendous amount of frustration built up." Listening to the warden and the articulate inmate make their counterpoints is an intriguing lesson in the disparate conclusions observers with opposing points of view can reach when assessing the same question. "There is a certain pettiness that runs rampant through certain members of the staff," complains the smuggler. "I'm talking the guards, because these are basically the people I'm in contact with. Fortunately for myself, I'm older than the average individual in here. As a consequence, my frustration level is probably less, simply because my maturity has given me the ability to cope with the whimsical behavior that we see prevalent in here."

He disagrees with the warden about the value of the educational opportunities at Collins Bay. "This particular institution here, we've come to realize, is simply nothing more than a warehouse. It's a revolving door. Here I am in here on a federal charge of marijuana and three ounces of cocaine, the transaction allegedly having occurred in Florida, and I have been given five years in a Canadian penitentiary on the cocaine charge alone. Now, when you look at it in total, doing nine years for two hundred pounds of marijuana and a three-ounce alleged transaction of cocaine that took place in my own country, but I'm arrested for here and put in prison for here because the alleged receiver of those three ounces of cocaine was allegedly a Canadian, then you start to think: Why the frustration? Why the resentment? Why men who are in here—who basically are uneducated and ill-equipped to handle the day-to-day challenges of society on the outside and are not taught really anything in this revolving-door institution – why are they ill-equipped when they go back out into society? And the answer is obvious."

But he wants to make sure his meaning is clear and continues, "What we have then is a system that is putting men inside that can't cope one way or the other in society and had to resort, to sustain themselves, to a robbery, a holdup, whatever. They are in here and are not really taught anything. Oh yes, there are education programs. Many of these people in here become frustrated with them, simply because they have not either the intellect nor the grade level to cope with the material presented."

We say our good-byes, and I walk out of Collins Bay, the electric gates grinding open along their tracks and then crashing shut with a slam of finality.

Life can be more complex for Americans locked up in Quebec. Collinsville Federal Penitentiary is about an hour's drive east of Montreal. I am escorted into the prison by a guard who speaks only French. Once inside, I meet with a black American inmate. Robert Downs is wearing a Redskins T-shirt and running shoes. "The only problems when you don't speak the language here," he says about his lack of fluency in French, "is if you have to have any type of administration business to take care of. Otherwise, as far as the prisoners are concerned, they have English-speaking and French-speaking prisoners here. So, as far as the population is concerned, it's not too much of a language barrier. But it's kind of hard to maneuver with the administration because there is a language barrier."

Downs was locked up for robbing a bank. He, too, was not interested in serving his time back home. "I saw that it wouldn't be too uncomfortable here." He even thought that not speaking French might make the time pass easier. "They speak their language and I speak my language and I wouldn't even have to communicate with them." But as he looks toward the end of his sentence, he realizes that the bank robbery wasn't his only mistake. "If I would have learned French I would have done much better time."

Medium security Collins Bay is adjacent to maximum security Millhaven in Kingston. There I find Anthony Vito Genavese, in for life, convicted of murder. "I've been up here for eleven years and I have also been in various prisons in the United States, federal and state, so serving the length of time that I'm serving, I sit back and find what is advantageous to me. Going back there, to their prison system, which is the federal prison system, or remaining in here in Canada within the federal system. Between the two, Canada far surpasses that of the United States."

At the top of the list of reasons is the smaller prison population in Canada. "That, I think, is an essential part of any type of correctional system that has to survive with the type of criminals that are entering the system now," he says in a quiet voice. He is wearing the prison "greens" issued at Millhaven. There are other factors that convinced him not to take advantage of the transfer treaty. "In Canada we don't have as many racial as well as ethnic-type differences that exist in the United States. Cliques, gangs, whatever you want to call them. That's part of the extensive problems that exist in the prisons in the United States; we don't have that in Canada. It boils down to being a matter of where you do your time best, and I find that I do my time better in Canada than in the United States."

Genavese doesn't believe his American citizenship has any bearing at all on his treatment by the police, the courts, or his jailers. His speech is an odd combination: he expresses the street smarts of a professional long-time criminal in a soft, clear erudite voice. "The shit was beaten out of me by the police, but that's something you expect, and it happens. That's their game and you just go along with it. If I had been in the States and picked up in Alabama I would be beaten ten times as hard as I was beaten up here. They're pussycats up here compared to some of the beatings down in Georgia and Alabama I've gotten or other people have gotten. They do it just a little bit more well-trained here. They don't show the marks. That's the only difference."

He's indifferent to the visits he gets from the U.S. consul. "I think I'm wasting their time, because they can't be of service to me at this time. At such time as I can use them, I'll let them know. I don't think that I'm being denied anything by being an American citizen and I'm not being given anything extra by being an American citizen. Unless somebody sees it on paper, they're not even aware of it. I'm not even familiar with all the Americans in here. So it's not like we're together like you would have in the States. The Canadians would be together. We don't have that up here, the Americans aren't all together. I don't even know how many we got up here in the institution and I know pretty well everybody."

Genavese has no patience with the argument that an American who violates the law overseas should get special consideration. "If an Ameri-

can citizen comes up into this country, or any country, he has to abide
by the laws of that particular country. Regardless of where it's at; Turkey, Iran, or wherever. I came up. I broke the law. And the law dealt
with it accordingly and they sentenced me. Okay, I'm accepting that. I
accepted that. Now leave me alone to do my time. That's my opinion,
that's my feeling about it. I'm paying for what I did. I'm not going to
cry to the American consulate or anybody else." He stops talking for a
second, and realizes the conditions where he is doing that time are pretty
comfortable. "Mind you, if I was in Turkey or something I probably
would be wanting to ring on his doorbell."

But Genavese is hesitant at first about calling Millhaven a country
club. "No, I definitely wouldn't call it that, not when you have killings
and suicides and whatnot left, right, and center. You can't say country
club. But I compare this to what I've been in before. Some people that
come here can't do that. They've only been here or they've been in other
prisons in Canada. I compare it to the worst of the worst that I've been
in. And to me, yes, it's a country club compared to the Alabama State
Penitentiary or Huntsville in Texas. It's a country club, of course."

One important difference he finds between Millhaven and the prisons
where he served in the United States is the opportunity for rehabilitation. "In the States you don't have time to learn. You're always on the
defensive. You're with your gang or with your clique and every move
that is made is defending your territorial bounds or plotting to go into
other territories – the hustles and manipulations and so forth. Here you
don't have that. So down there I couldn't have the time to think and do
art like I do up here and writing. But up here, that's all I do. I have that
time because that problem doesn't exist here."

Before the visit ends, there's time for a moment of patriotism. "I'm
an American. I always will be an American. I'm proud to be from the
United States of America. But I like Canada, too. I only wish that I
would have used a little common sense prior to all this nonsense and
come up here legally and lived legally because it's a beautiful country.
But I do miss the States. Oh, yeah. Of course. I mean, like from New
York to Los Angeles – you have anything in the United States. I've always liked it. I always will."

Another electric gate scrapes shut and I glance back at Millhaven, and
its guard towers and wire-topped stone walls.

Stay out of Trouble

> First, he must have some entrance into the language
> before he goeth. Then he must have such a servant
> or tutor as knoweth the country. Let him carry with
> him also some card or book describing the country
> where he travelleth.
>
> Sir Francis Bacon, offering advice to travelers
> in his 1625 essay *Of Travel*

> Between 6 and 7 million U.S. citizens visit Mexico
> each year, while more than 400,000 Americans re-
> side there. Although the majority thoroughly enjoy
> their stay, some experience difficulties and serious
> inconvenience.
>
> U.S. State Department booklet
> *Tips for Travelers to Mexico*

||||||||||||||||||| **A**s Gene LePere and her Turkish nightmare show, as the tales of long and miserable investigative detentions make clear, as the cultural mistakes of American oil workers in Saudi Arabia or the business miscalculations of a Richard Flynn or a Marie McBroom indicate, almost anyone is vulnerable to the misery of foreign incarceration. With several thousand Americans imprisoned overseas at any one time, and with several thousand arrested every year, it is a problem that can easily touch any of us.

Should Americans—even those who anticipate breaking no laws—never leave home? Of course not. As Billy Hayes says with the unfortunate credibility that comes from his hard-earned experience, "You should know what you're doing." All the privileges, all the rights of U.S. citizenship mean nothing when foreign police drag an American off to a miserable jail filled with violent criminals who don't speak English. The U.S. government usually cannot get Americans out of foreign jails, often doesn't particularly want to release them, or doesn't want to jeopardize international relations for just one unfortunate prisoner. And prisoners shouldn't expect to be able to buy their way out of jail. A corrupt, primitive prison system doesn't mean bribes usually work, and brazen escape is rarely successful.

Simple mistakes are easy to make in foreign cultures, and can lead to a prison cell. One of the reasons Americans are susceptible to arrest and imprisonment is because we are spoiled by the relative fairness of our own judicial system. Although there certainly are egregious exceptions, for the most part the innocent are not kept in jail for long here, and even the guilty enjoy the benefits of a legal system that presumes innocence until that guilt is proven beyond a reasonable doubt.

One of my early overseas reporting trips took me to Yemen. During a break in my work schedule, I ambled down to the Cable and Wireless telephone office in Sana'a and placed a collect call to my wife in California. We talked leisurely, catching up on the past several days since I left home. Once we hung up, I headed out the door of the office only to be flagged down by the clerk and presented with a bill.

"Oh no," I waved the invoice away. "I called collect; they paid at the other end of the line."

The clerk was insistent. Not only had I not called collect, at the time it seemed it wasn't even possible to call collect from Yemen to America. I was faced with the bill again and translated it from riyals; it came to about one hundred dollars. Luckily I had a wad of traveler's checks in my pocket. But what if I hadn't? I certainly didn't know the law in Yemen at the time. Is it fraud to place a call and then not have the money? What would the telephone company do to a customer who hung up the phone but couldn't pay, even if there was no intent to default on the bill? They would probably call the police, it would likely be considered theft, and the caller could easily wind up in a dank cell for the error of not clearly communicating with the clerk before the call was placed.

I know I made it clear I wanted to call collect. Looking back on the scene, I can only imagine that the clerk understood nothing of what I was requesting and simply ignored my chatter about reversing the charges. It was probably such a foreign concept to him that it was easier for him to just move on to the business at hand: making the connection to California.

Similar mistakes and miscalculations are part of the daily baggage of world travel. Cautious travelers should double-check the terms before entering into even the most routine business transactions.

Other types of mistakes are easier to avoid. When I bounced up that dirt road toward the Turkish and Soviet Armenian border for a look down at earthquake-destroyed Leninakan, I knew I was taking a risk. The reason I was on the dirt road in the first place was because the border crossing was closed. Travel at the time between Turkey and the Soviet Union was seriously restricted. Efficient travelers skilled in survival techniques know that a tense political border usually means some sort of restricted zone, where trespassing often results in arrest. My excuse was that my job takes me to dangerous places. I knew approaching the border was risky; I just incorrectly assumed I could talk the soldiers into letting me take a look.

Years before I found myself wandering around the Turkish-Soviet border, a young American named Newcomb Mott was arrested in Murmansk because a border guard caught him traveling without the proper visa for that region of the Soviet Union. He was sentenced to eighteen months in prison and died – supposedly it was a suicide – on the train to where his confinement was to take place.*

The notes I took reporting on the Armenian earthquake show how easy it is to make a border miscalculation:

After turning around at military control signs on the main road near the border point, I made my way up a winding dirt track to a point that looked likely to offer a view down to Leninakan.

I drove toward a building that looked military and hoped I hadn't somehow inadvertently missed a Turkish checkpoint and was instead coming up on a Soviet one. I passed an empty sentry hut – slowly to make sure I did not appear to be a threat or appear to be attempting to run through a demand to stop. Then I was relieved to see the familiar larger-than-life gold-colored head of Ataturk. It meant I was still on the Turkish side. I stopped and strode with a wide smile toward the building.

"Hello," I called. I was still smiling and I stretched my hand out to the first shocked soldier. I was immediately quite sure – from his

*Mott's story is briefly cited in the 1967 Maurice Hindus book *The Kremlin's Human Dilemma: Russia after Half a Century of Revolution,* published by Doubleday.

surprised response—that I had breached some serious security. The soldier waved me away with rapid Turkish that I made clear I could not understand.

So he walked me over to a perimeter sign I had missed seeing as I drove up the rutted road. It forbade coming closer than 300 yards from the border.

I looked down at Leninakan—too hazy and far away to appear in distress—and watched planes take off and land. The Turks patrolled their side by looking into the clouds when they thought they heard an encroaching aircraft.

Two cups of tea and an offer of breakfast later, the crackling radios and the marginal English of one of the soldiers made it clear I was no longer a free man.

A soldier strapped on his pistol and got

That's where my notes end. I can't remember if I kept writing and lost the notes, or never finished. But I do remember what happened next.

The soldier got into my rented car, adjusted his gun, and drove with me, stern-faced, away from the border. We returned to the little village where I'd spent the night. I stopped the car, at his insistence, in front of the army fort in the village and said an optimistic, "Good-bye!"

But it wasn't going to be so easy. He insisted that I go inside to the commander with him. They exchanged words that I could not understand. I made it clear that I needed to use the telephone.

Together we walked a block or so through the dusty village streets to the post office. I placed a call to the U.S. embassy in Ankara and explained my predicament. A Turkish-speaking embassy employee got on the line with my soldier and then told me the good news. I was simply being escorted, firmly, far from the border. Hoping the interpretation was correct, I got back in the car. So did my soldier, and we headed back toward Kars.

About halfway there we turned into a heavily fortified military camp. Tanks and artillery were everywhere; soldiers were training, shooting, and running obstacle courses. Together we tramped to the commander's office. It was jammed with villagers who appeared to be petitioning for help, gossiping, or just keeping warm next to his stove. Finally, from the commander, I heard some clear English.

I was admonished for violating the security zone, and told to head back to Kars. "Gladly," I responded, asking if I could leave my armed passenger at the fort.

"Of course," the commander bellowed his reply, laughing, "we are not Russians!"

The lesson is obvious. Stay away from military installations; watch for restrictions around borders. Learn the basic commands in the local language that probably mean trouble if violated, words that appear on warning signs or are shouted by authority figures: *stop, forbidden, no, restricted, danger*. Watch for those signs, both literal and conceptual. The onus is on the traveler to stay out of trouble, not the other way around. The foreign culture and government are not going to second-guess an American's ignorance or naiveté. It is up to the traveler to try to understand the often subtle clues and cues that mean stop, forbidden, no, restricted, danger.

Language provides some access into cultural differences, and spending just a short time with a primary phrase book and a dictionary can prevent serious later misunderstandings. Often basic grunts and gestures – that might seem universally understandable to those uninitiated in the diversity of world cultures – mean something insulting or opposite to what an American wants to communicate. My favorite example is the nod of the head for yes, the shake of the head for no. Those are clear, even automatic methods of communicating for Americans, unambiguous. But in the Balkans, those signs are reversed. The nod means no, the shake means yes. Imagine the trouble not knowing that difference could cause at a time of crisis, when split-second decisions are being made by young, poorly trained police and soldiers. Why would it even occur to them that the foreigner they are dealing with wouldn't know something as basic as what a nod and a shake of the head mean?

A wise traveler quickly learns a basic vocabulary of emergency words and phrases – *no, yes, please, I'm sorry, telephone, I don't speak your language, I speak English* – key words to make as clear as possible that no damage was intended and that help is needed.

Caution should be exercised when taking photographs. What constitutes a tourist snapshot back home can easily be construed as spying elsewhere. Without gaining express permission, avoid taking pictures of military installations, international borders, airports, railroad stations, even anyone in a uniform. Many paranoid regimes frown on any photography of their infrastructure. That includes such seemingly (by American standards) innocuous subject matters as bridges and electric power stations.

Binoculars, often just an innocent tool for bird watchers in the United States, look like espionage equipment to many foreign police inspectors. Leave them home unless you really need them. Any extra baggage that can be misinterpreted as improper is best left behind. The less professional cameras, computers, and recording equipment look, the less grief they usually cause. Basically, devices that appear to be common tourist equipment tend to get across borders and past checkpoints with the least delay.

Americans tend toward arrogance. We have a propensity to walk with a John Wayne swagger through the world. On occasion that can get us out of a jam; it is possible to force oneself past an intimidated foreign authority. But often, especially these days, such an attitude can be counterproductive. A policeman in some little dictatorship just might figure he'll get an extra notch in his belt if he brings in an American. The relative success of the hostage-takers in Lebanon was a lesson that Americans can be vulnerable and impotent.

Under most circumstances, adopting a loud "Don't-mess-with-me-I'm-an-American" attitude is no help during a personal crisis. I've tried it with the East German highway police and found it counterproductive. Americans should leave chips on the shoulder at home. Authority is much less pliant in most other parts of the world than it is in the United States.

Besides international border crossings, one of the most likely places to encounter police is in traffic. Travelers should seriously consider the potential for problems before sliding behind the wheel of an automobile in a foreign country. Not only are rules of the road often different from the norms at home, but other drivers and hazards like livestock on the highways and miserable road maintenance may create difficult driving conditions. Accidents and routine encounters with traffic police are common. The result of these encounters can easily be jail for the driver.

Trains, buses, and shared taxis provide safe and congenial alternatives to driving in most of the world. If a traveler is intent on making use of a private car, the easiest method of avoiding most problems on the road is to hire a chauffeur. Either take taxis, or find a taxi driver with a decent car who wants to make some extra money and will hire himself out on a long-term basis. The rates are usually competitive with renting a car to drive yourself. Aside from eliminating most of the headaches of driving, hiring a car and driver means hiring a traveling companion, too. The traveler who takes some care in choosing a driver can end up with a friend, but perhaps much more important for the success of a trip is to pick a driver who speaks adequate English. Then the traveler gets a car, driver, companion, translator, and guide. It's much better than driving off into the unknown alone in a rented car.

A terrifying example of how dangerous driving can be for a foreigner occurred in Moscow after the Soviet Union crumbled. In the relative void of power and structure that followed, the new entrepreneurs in Russia included the traffic police. I didn't need to worry about them; I hired a car and driver. Pavel charged fifty dollars a month for his services as a guide and driver, the use of his aging Lada, and all the gasoline we needed.

On the streets of Moscow, every few hundred yards, a traffic cop is stationed. Even in the worst winter weather the police are out, bundled up in thick greatcoats, their heads covered with traditional Russian fur caps. Eyeing the passing traffic carefully, they look for foreign license plates and foreign-looking drivers. Once in a while, bored, they would wave Pavel and me over to the side of the road. He would get out into the cold and pull his car papers and driver's license out of his wallet, talking fast in an imploring, explaining, apologetic voice. He never received a ticket while we were together. Then he would get back into the car, shake his head, and mutter "*Yasha,*" with disgust – derogatory taxi driver slang for cop.

Life on the Moscow streets isn't so easy for the foreign drivers stopped by these *yasha.* By early 1992, they were demanding one hundred dollars (not a hundred dollars' worth of rubles, but one hundred U.S. dollars) in cash for supposed violations of Moscow's traffic laws. Irritated drivers who consider refusing to pay the extortion are then threatened with a trip to the police station and a blood alcohol test. Drunk driving is a serious crime in Russia. The police are notorious for drawing the blood samples with dirty needles; foreign drivers understandably worried about AIDS and other diseases cough up the hundred dollars rather than submit to the tests. Such problems are avoided by hiring local drivers.

Skillful travelers seeking to minimize the possible problems with foreign judicial systems keep in close touch with the current history of the lands they visit. Good guidebooks that pull no punches are essential. The guidebook industry is responding to more adventurous travelers by publishing much more thorough and candid guides. Lonely Planet maintains a solid list of detailed and blunt editions offering specific advice for some of the more remote ports of call in the world. *The South American Handbook*, updated annually, is justly famous for its straightforward approach to the dangers that can ambush the unwary traveler.

There are plenty of worthless guidebooks on the market that show tempting pictures of a faraway destination and suggest a few hotels to stay in and some intriguing folkloric trinkets to bring home. Their value is marginal; such books can serve to remind travelers about landmarks they want to visit but they won't do much to expose unexpected dangers on the road. An example of the vital information provided by a decent guide can be found right at the beginning of *The South American Handbook*. Under the heading "Law Enforcement" is this sobering passage:

Whereas in Europe and North America we are accustomed to law enforcement on a systematic basis, in general, enforcement in Latin America is achieved by periodic campaigns. The most typical is a round-up of criminals in the cities just before Christmas. In December, therefore, you may well be asked for identification at any time, and if you cannot produce it, you will be jailed. At first sight, on arrival, it may seem that you can flout the law with impunity, because everybody else is doing so. If a visitor is jailed his friends should take him food every day. This is especially important for people on a diet, such as diabetics. It must be borne in mind that in the event of a vehicle accident in which anyone is injured, all drivers involved are automatically detained until blame has been established, and this does not usually take less than two weeks. Sometimes these problems can be avoided by offering a bribe, but this, naturally, is illegal and may be extremely dangerous.

Never offer a bribe unless you are fully conversant with the customs of the country. Wait until the official makes the suggestion, or offer money in some form which is apparently not bribery, e.g., "In our country we have a system of on-the-spot fines. Is there a similar system here?" Do not assume that an official who accepts a bribe is prepared to do anything else that is illegal. You bribe him to persuade him to do his job, or to persuade him not to do it, or to do it more quickly, or more slowly. You do not bribe him to do something which is against the law. The mere suggestion would make him very upset.*

It is definitely worth the trouble to seek such valuable information about laws and law enforcement before traveling. But ideal guidebooks do not exist for all destinations. There are alternative devices to turn to for guidance. One trick is to use the guide to a neighboring and similar country, then expect the worst. Such caution will probably be rewarded with a reduced likelihood of trouble with the local authorities.

One of the best sources of current information is a recent traveler. Never be shy about asking questions from other travelers. Whatever satisfaction might be derived from pretending to be experienced and worldly cannot compete with the value of the latest reports from the scene. Before leaving home try to find an expert who has just returned and grill him or her about what to expect in the field. This is a technique that should be used consistently during a trip. On the airplane, ask fellow passengers if this is their first journey to the destination. Keep asking until a veteran is found. Seasoned and sophisticated travelers won't only share ideas and experiences about minimizing problems with officials, they can also offer practical information about entertaining places to go and things to do that might be missing from incomplete guidebooks.

Similarly, the U.S. government should be utilized by travelers. Although in busier cities embassy and consulate staffs often will be preoccupied and won't want to be bothered, the atmosphere can be the reverse in out-of-the-way postings. There, a call to a consular officer may well result in a full-scale briefing about the country in question, filled with advice about how to stay out of trouble. Whatever political party might be in the White House, these career consular officers can usually be relied upon to offer a fair and detailed, if official, account of how the American government perceives the local scene.

The U.S. government and its agents overseas do not want American citizens to get into trouble. The worst aspect of such official briefings may be that the consular officers are too cautious and try to rein in a traveler's natural adventurous spirit. In addition, U.S. citizens traveling

---

The South American Handbook is published by Trade & Travel Publications in Bath, England, and distributed in the United States by Prentice-Hall Travel. It is expensive but worth every penny.

in questionable locales are encouraged by their government to register with the closest American mission. Theoretically, the government will get in touch with registered Americans if changing conditions warrant such a contact. Similarly, if a registered American disappears, a foreign service officer may be inclined to make some inquiries.

Even in posts where the diplomats are too busy to offer casual briefings, valuable information is available from the U.S. embassy or consulate. Diplomatic posts include an office called American Citizen Services. With just a telephone call, specific questions about safety and security, and local laws and customs, usually can be answered. The American Citizen Services officer will be prepared to offer broad suggestions about what types of activities and places to stay away from to avoid trouble.

Another worthwhile offering from the U.S. government is the State Department travel advisory. Typically, advisories identify countries where crime is a crisis, governments are particularly unfriendly to U.S. citizens, or civil unrest is severe. Travel advisories also identify places where contact with dangerous diseases is likely, or basic survival services are difficult to obtain. Information about changes in laws, such as those governing visas, can also be found in these advisories.

Citations from some old travel advisories suggest the type of crucial information that can be found in them. For example: "A curfew enforced by the government of Suriname is in effect Sunday through Thursday from 12 A.M. to 4 A.M. Curfew is not in force on Friday and Saturday nights." Such specifics about when it is legal to be out on the streets are vital. Travelers to Colombia were warned in another advisory, "No road traffic is permitted through Guajira from 6 P.M. until 6 A.M. It is not advisable to travel after hours of darkness as bandits dressed as police officials are known to stop and rob persons traveling in vehicles." Those intending to visit Ghana would have been well served by a warning to stay away except for essential reasons and that "A number of foreigners, including U.S. citizens, have been detained occasionally without being informed of charges against them or without notification by the government of Ghana to the arrested individuals' embassy. In addition, some travelers arriving and departing Kotoka International Airport in Accra have been subject to body searches and private correspondence has been opened. Tourist photography and undeveloped film carried by travelers out of the country are suspect. Travelers are urged to practice the utmost prudence in taking pictures anywhere in Ghana and to avoid taking pictures anywhere in Accra." From a travel advisory for Pakistan came this warning, "There is a ban on travel in the Khyber Agency, which in practice means the Khyber Pass."

These official alerts are valuable additions to any traveler's baggage whether or not they are followed, and can be found at passport offices, requested by mail from the State Department, or heard over the telephone by calling the State Department's Citizens Emergency Center in Washington, D.C. Compuserve and other electronic bulletin boards now carry the messages. They can be found in the Official Airlines Guide database, and now are transmitted routinely to most airlines, mass media outlets, and many American private companies doing business overseas.

More general travel suggestions can be found in other government publications. The State Department Bureau of Consular Affairs stays quite current with its *Tips for Travelers* series. For example, in *Tips for Travelers to Eastern Europe,* potential problems that might face travelers in each of the former Soviet bloc countries are introduced. "Except for personal use," the 1991 edition explains about Albanian policy, "it is forbidden to bring religious items, such as Bibles or Korans, into the country." Hungarian law, it says, holds that "Most art and antiques, even if they are family possessions, cannot be exported without a permit." The booklet warns travelers: "Be aware that undercover police may offer to exchange money on the black market. Americans have been arrested in Hungary for attempting such transactions."

A few words are probably in order here about breaking the law. Professional criminals are on their own, as are spies. They come to business-based conclusions about such matters. But all other travelers must regularly make moral and practical decisions about whether or not to bend and break laws, both at home and abroad. The black market is an ideal example. It is often easy to get a better currency exchange rate on the street than is offered in the banks. The advice the U.S. government offers to travelers to Hungary is valid. For the average traveler, the amount of money saved by using the illegal black market is rarely worth the risk. This is also a moral, ethical, and political choice; using the black market in a country struggling to establish a successful economy is counterproductive to such efforts. But if the decision is made to exchange money outside the legal apparatus, travelers should follow a cautious path.

Enough money should be exchanged legally so that authorities can be presented with paperwork proving that the traveler did not ignore currency restrictions. Such a legal exchange also makes it unnecessary to rush into the black market. The traveler can then take the time to choose a trusted black marketeer, usually a taxi driver or someone else with whom other financial and social interactions are taking place. A sleazy-looking man on a street corner, in a shabby trench coat, carrying a thick roll of bills, is not a good choice.

The same common sense applies to other decisions about whether or not to break local laws. Take the time and effort to make a basic risk-benefit assessment. Usually the most practical conclusion is to obey the local laws.

It is important to understand the spirit, not just the letter, of the law. If a traveler, for example, enters a country on a tourist visa, grievous complications can ensue if the host government determines that the visa was violated because some sort of commerce was conducted by the tourist. The burden is on the careful traveler to know the details of visa restrictions.

So many dangers, so many uncertainties make some Americans afraid to travel the world, but staying at home to avoid the risks of travel is unnecessarily paranoid. Millions of Americans are on the international roads every day with no trouble. Many of them employ just a little common sense and caution to increase their odds of catching their flight back to the United States with no unwanted postponement.

The collapse of Communist governments reminds us how quickly the opposition can become the government, how quickly governments can go out of business. The difference between a terrorist and a freedom fighter often rests upon a political or philosophical interpretation of the motives of these warriors. Because distinctions between political enemies and political friends may be nebulous, those concerned with self-preservation often try to travel with as stateless an appearance as possible. No matter how much of a flag-waving patriot one may be, advertising allegiance to America and American citizenship is not always the best route for safe travel. Arbitrary arrest and imprisonment may well be avoided by blending into the crowd.

That does not mean that a traveler acts ashamed to be an American. It is merely an acceptance of the reality that lowering one's profile usually increases survivability. Basically, leave at home those things that advertise Americanism: baseball caps promoting American companies;

Redskins T-shirts; red, white, and blue jogging outfits. Keep voices displaying American accents at a low volume in public places.

By entering a foreign culture as anonymously as possible, a traveler sets at least some of the terms for interaction; anti-American prejudice can be defused. By shedding overt and stereotypical American behavior, travelers are able to avoid sticking out like a sore thumb.

The preceding is not meant to be an intimidating list of precautions. Rather, the intent is to offer logical suggestions that are easy to miss during the crush of preparations for a trip overseas and easy to forget during a fast-paced foreign adventure. Remember, the odds of being arrested overseas are statistically low.

Should Americans fear leaving home? Again, of course not. Just learn the local laws, and know the possible consequences of actions. Life offers no guarantees.

No Picnic at Home

The choice is clear. More prison space
or more crime.

U.S. Attorney General William Barr

|||||||||||||||||||||| **D**espite the horrors of many prisons abroad, it's important to remember how vile prison conditions often remain in the United States, and how disturbingly large America's prison population has grown. These facts reflect an unacceptable social blight, a tainting of the American dream that must be factored into any condemnation of foreign customs, police, courts, and prisons.

It's the job of another book, or a library full of books, to report on the nightmares of the American criminal justice system and the social fiascoes that contribute to the escalating U.S. prison population. But noting a few of the depressing numbers makes clear that a crisis exists at home.

After the remarkable revolutions in 1989, the Soviet Union and South Africa released large numbers of political prisoners. That left the United States of America in the sad role of leading the world in the ratio of prisoners to population. An organization called the Sentencing Project* keeps track of these statistics. Their latest figures are shocking. In most of the rest of the world, average rates of imprisonment are rarely

---

*The Sentencing Project identifies itself as "a national non-profit organization which promotes sentencing reform and conducts research on criminal justice issues." Its 1991 report on the rate of imprisonment in America is titled, *Americans Behind Bars: A Comparison of International Rates of Incarceration.* That report was followed by a 1992 edition called *Americans Behind Bars: One Year Later.* Both are available from the Sentencing Project, 918 F Street NW, Suite 501, Washington, DC 20004.

higher than 100 citizens incarcerated for every 100,000 in the general
population.

Except for a few statistically inconsequential small nations, the
United States leaves those average rates in the dust. In 1989, the U.S.
rate was 426 prisoners incarcerated for every 100,000 citizens in the
general population. One year later that figure jumped to 455 for each
100,000. A look back shows a failing society. In the decade since 1980,
the number of prisoners in the United States doubled. The number is
three times the figure for 1973. Of course, even with all these prison inmates, crime continues to plague America. Although most U.S. prisons
are free of the more wretched conditions that exist overseas, they are too
often filled with despair and violence. Worse, for society, they are
efficient training grounds not for rehabilitation, but for criminality.

The attorney general is wrong; the choice is not just between more
cells and crime.* The choice includes determining why—especially
when compared with so much of the rest of the world—American society
produces so many criminals. Once that question is answered, it would
be wise to figure out how to reverse the trend.

---

*Attorney General Barr made his call for "more prison space" on January 14, 1992,
in a speech to the California District Attorneys Association.

Select Bibliography

Midnight Express (Dutton, 1977) is Billy Hayes's story, written with William Hoffer. The book, and the Oliver Stone movie script that followed, became the gauge many American travelers used to judge foreign prisons. "This is no *Midnight Express,*" the American consul in Bangkok told me about the conditions for Americans in prisons there, and I heard prisoners and lawyers describe conditions in places as disparate as Peru and Pakistan as, "just like *Midnight Express.*"

One of Billy Hayes's lawyers was Michael Griffith, a member of the International Legal Defense Counsel, the group of lawyers that specializes in representing Americans imprisoned overseas. ILDC offers the following publications for readers who want specific legal information and suggestions for dealing with being arrested and held in a foreign country.

The Hassle of Your Life: A Handbook for Families of Americans Incarcerated Abroad is an overview for those facing the crisis.

As the title implies, *Coming Home: A Handbook for Americans Imprisoned in Mexico* provides information for those locked up just south of the border. Along with a thorough assessment of the transfer treaty, authors Robert Fogelnest, Theodore Simon, and Robert Pisani offer this philosophical pat on the back to returning American prisoners, "No doubt you will have acquired some personal insight due to the ordeal you have gone through, and hopefully this will have contributed to making you a stronger person."

Repatriation: A Handbook for Americans Imprisoned in Europe offers an analysis of the Council of Europe's prisoner transfer treaty.

A technical overview of existing transfer treaties and a look at those being considered and negotiated can be found in *The United States Treaties on Transfer of Prisoners,* which is reprinted from the *Pacific Law Journal.*

The ILDC booklets are available from the law firm directly, at this address:

> 24th Floor Packard Building
> 111 South 15th Street
> Philadelphia, PA 19102

Another ILDC client, Gene LePere, tells her story in *Never Pass This Way Again* (Adler & Adler, 1987).

Gerald Amster describes his failed smuggling trip in *Transit Point Moscow: The True Story of an American's Imprisonment in a Soviet Gulag and His Astonishing Escape* (Holt, Rinehart & Winston, 1984). Amster's coauthor is Bernard Asbell, who writes in an afterword that he's convinced the "adventure happened exactly as he's told it." It is one of the least believable "nonfiction" books I've ever read.

Ken Follet's account of H. Ross Perot's adventures in Iran is detailed in *On the Wings of Eagles* (William Morrow, 1983). "This is a true story about a group of people who, accused of crimes they did not commit, decided to make their own justice," writes Follet. What Follet neglects to mention in his book, which was reissued and sold well during the 1992 presidential campaign, is that he guaranteed editorial control of his manuscript to Perot in return for access to the story.

Missing, the terrifying story of the execution of American journalist Charles Horman, is difficult to find. The Thomas Hauser book was last published by Avon in 1982 and is out of print. The Costa-Gavras film based on the book, also titled *Missing,* is available on videotape cassette. Jack Lemmon's performance as the father who loses faith in his government is sobering.

From the U.S. State Department Bureau of Consular Affairs a variety of pamphlets are available free, including these:

Crisis Abroad – What the State Department Does (Department of State Publication 9732) provides a rudimentary overview.

Travel Warning on Drugs Abroad (Department of State Publication 9558) is just that, with a sobering listing of what the U.S. consular officer can and cannot do. "DON'T LET YOUR TRIP BECOME A NIGHTMARE!" warns the booklet. It lists the telephone numbers of the Citizens Emergency Center, the official connection between an arrested American and interested friends and family.

The "Crossing the Border" section of the *AAA Travel Guide to Mexico* makes sobering reading. It is available at local AAA clubs to members or from the association's offices: 1000 AAA Drive, Heathrow, FL 32746–5063.

For more general travel information to less traveled destinations, a whole series of booklets is available from the U.S. Government Printing Office for one dollar each. These are titled *Tips for Travelers* and include some of the more sensitive destinations in the world, from sub-Saharan Africa to the Middle East.

Addresses to Write and Visit

After inspecting the cases of many of the Americans in foreign jails, other Americans can breathe a long sigh of relief and realize, "That easily could have been me instead."

Such a response might prompt traveling Americans to consider taking an afternoon off now and again to visit their countrymen and women held behind foreign bars. Usually visits for these unfortunates are rare. Almost always they appreciate the diversion of a short chat, some fresh food, and a few recent English-language periodicals and books. Similarly, pen pal relationships generally are relished by the inmates.

A few years ago I was in La Paz, Bolivia, working on a story about cocaine trafficking and discovered that the prison there housed a handful of Americans. A friend and I paid them a short visit. They were miserable: depressed, frustrated with their lot in life, guilty of drug smuggling attempts, and underfed. We listened to their complaints and anguish for a while and then they slunk back into the oppressive depths of San Pedro Prison. We came back later with a couple of bags of groceries: tinned meats and fresh yogurt, some fruits and vegetables. They were thrilled by the dietary supplements. And it made us feel good to help.

Addresses of specific prisons where Americans are incarcerated are readily available from American embassies and consulates or from the State Department Bureau of Consular Affairs in Washington. It is impossible to obtain the name and address of a specific prisoner unless the inmate signs a Privacy Act waiver. The following select list includes a few prisons on many American travelers' itineraries where the population might well include Americans happy to see visitors from home. Remember that visitors to many, if not most, prisons, must expect to be searched for contraband and should bring passports for identification.

Carcel Nacional La Modelo
Cr #56A 19–30
Bogotá, Colombia

M.A. Paris la Santé
42, rue de la Santé
75674 Paris Cedex 14, France

JVA Frankfurt
Obere Kreuzackstrasse 8
6000 Frankfurt 50, Germany

Athens Men's Prison
Korydallos
Athens 18110, Greece

Aguada Central Jail
Sinquirim Bardez
Goa 403515, India

Fort Augusta Correctional
Centre
St. Catherines
Kingston, Jamaica

Prison Civil à Tangiers
Tangiers, Morocco

Bhadraghol Jail
Kendriya Karagor
Kathmandu, Nepal

Penitaire Inrictingen Overamstel
Hje Wenckebachweg 48
1096 An Amsterdam,
Netherlands

C.P. Algeciras
Cadiz, Spain

Klong Prem Prison
33/2 Ngam Wong Wan Road,
Bangkhen
Bangkok 10 900, Thailand

Information for this partial list came from the organization Prisoners Abroad, a British group founded in 1978 expressly for the purpose of working, as its literature explains, "for the welfare and interests of Britons, or people who have close links with our country, who are detained overseas." There is no equivalent group operating in the United States. Prisoners Abroad connects prisoners with pen pals, publishes a quarterly newsletter, and engages in a wide variety of campaigns to actively help individual prisoners. The group can be reached at:
        82 Rosebery Avenue
        London EC1R 4RR, England

Amnesty International works with American prisoners who meet their criteria for clients: political prisoners and victims of torture. The organization's main U.S. address is:

304 West 58th Street
New York, NY 10019

Note on Terminology

By its very nature, this is a book that focuses on nationality. It is about citizens of the United States of America in trouble away from their homeland. Under ideal circumstances, humanity might coexist as one big happy global family. Such is obviously not the case, and one of the artificial divisions we have created that most affects our fates and day-to-day lives is that of nationality.

When I write about "foreign" countries, the word *foreign* is intended to carry no derogatory connotations. It does not imply that governments and cultures other than those of the United States are abnormal, improper, unnatural, irrelevant, or in any way inferior. I use the term *foreign* in the purely political sense: a place removed from one's native nation, mine being the USA.

I use the word *American* to mean a citizen of the United States of America. Yes, I know that such usage is frowned upon in some circles. I am aware that, technically, the entire Western Hemisphere is America and its inhabitants all Americans. But for simple convenience I accept as reality that one of the effects of cultural imperialism over the last few hundred years has been an appropriation of the word *American* by us gringos. Like it or not, we, and most of the rest of the world, call people from the United States Americans, while those from directly south of our border, for example, are internationally referred to as Mexicans. It may not be linguistically fair, but the term communicates and I use it for its commonly accepted meaning.

All the names, titles, places, charges, and crimes cited in this book are factual. When a person did not want his or her real name to be used or I felt this could inappropriately compromise the individual's safety or future, I simply omitted the name from the story.

Acknowledgments

This book, like most, profits from the help of a wide range of friends, acquaintances, and colleagues. But it would have been much more difficult to produce without the bold and imaginative leadership Jim Farley practiced when he headed the NBC radio division news department. This was before General Electric bought the network and gutted radio from NBC's operations. When, as a news correspondent assigned to NBC's Washington bureau, I went to New York and marched into Farley's Rockefeller Center office suggesting a trip around the world to interview Americans in prisons, he asked me a few key questions about the project and then demanded, "When can you leave?"

Bob Dore produced the documentary that resulted from that research trip, and I thank him for both his hard work and the security he offered as I made my way into one prison hellhole after another in strange lands. I knew that if I failed to call in after a faraway interview, Dore would use all the resources he could muster to fetch me home.

Lawyers Richard Atkins and Theodore Simon, partners in the International Legal Defense Counsel firm, were gracious about sharing their time, files, and contacts and I thank them.

During my journey around the world, I was debilitated by the time I reached Thailand with some stomach trouble that I traced to a Mongolian barbecue in Hong Kong. My friends Heather and Eric Nadel nursed me back to health at their home in India, and for that I am tremendously appreciative.

Colleagues around the world provided invaluable assistance. Several fellow news reporters helped by conducting interviews for the project or extending advice and counsel. These include Neil Davis, who offered his expertise as guidance for me in Thailand; Rick Espinosa, who shared his familiarity with Tijuana and joined me for the La Mesa visit; Randall Lyman, who insisted to the new Czech government that their prisons be open to reporters; and Mitch Lebe, who gathered needed information in New York City. My friend Chris Kojm efficiently helped me extricate some needed statistical information from the tedious U.S. government bureaucracy. And my late friend Don Chamberlain was a valuable critic for the work in progress.

Back in California after field reporting, the calm of my studio at the Headlands Center for the Arts provided a bucolic counterpoint for writing and editing, the view of the Pacific only slightly distracting. My thanks to Jennifer Dowley, the director at the Headlands, and her staff and the board, for making the center the oasis that it is.

As always, I benefit from the support of my family. I can trace my interviewing skills to my mother, Eva Laufer, and my wanderlust to my father, Thomas Laufer. My sons, Talmage Morris and Michael Laufer, tendered enthusiastic encouragement as work progressed. My wife, Sheila Swan Laufer, provided her usual tireless feedback, advice, and sustenance.

I wish to thank my editors, Thomas Christensen and David Peattie, publisher William Brinton, and all the staff at Mercury House for their vision.

It would have been impossible to reflect the plight of these incarcerated Americans had not so many agreed to speak with me. For that I am appreciative, but I know that the exchange was a fair one. Those with whom I spoke in foreign prisons were glad for the visit and a sympathetic ear. Those who told their tales back home after their release found it therapeutic to air their memories one more time. And I dare say all of them hoped that publicizing their nightmares abroad will warn fellow travelers to be discreet and vigilant, wary and watchful, especially far from home.

About the Author

Photo: Philip Wyatt

Peter Laufer is the author of *Iron Curtain Rising: A Personal Journey through the Changing Landscape of Eastern Europe,* for which he was first runner-up for the Lowell Thomas Travel Journalism Award. He won the Long Island University George Polk Award and Ohio State and American Bar Association awards for his NBC radio documentary on Americans imprisoned overseas, the impetus for *Nightmare Abroad.*

For many years, Laufer has traveled throughout the world as a free-lance radio and newspaper reporter. He has worked as an NBC News correspondent from its Washington bureau, reported extensively for the ABC radio network, and covered revolutions and elections in Eastern Europe as well as the Gulf War for CBS radio. His reports on other major news stories such as the war in Nicaragua, cocaine trafficking in South America, and the AIDS epidemic also have been widely published and have brought him several Society of Professional Journalists, B'nai B'rith Edward R. Murrow, and National Headliner awards.

Laufer lives in Marin County, California, with his wife and two sons.

The text of this book was designed by Zipporah Collins. The type is Plantin with Stymie display. Typesetting was done by Stanton Publication Services. The copyeditor was Mary Lou Carlson. Production was coordinated by Hazel White. The book is printed on 50-pound Lindenmeyr Antique, an acid-free, recycled paper. Printing and binding were done by R. R. Donnelley and Sons.